D1172843

My Hand in His

Ancient Truths in Modern Parables

By Herman W. Gockel

CONCORDIA PUBLISHING HOUSE

SAINT LOUIS, MISSOURI

Concordia Publishing House, St. Louis 18, Mo.
Concordia Publishing House Ltd., London, W. C. 1
Copyright 1961 by Concordia Publishing House

Library of Congress Catalog Card No. 60-15577

Preface

There are two statements in the Gospel According to St. Mark which, while they are separated by eight chapters, are nevertheless closely related to each other. The first is written in the fourth chapter where we are told of Jesus: "And with many *parables* spake He the Word unto them, as they were able to hear it. But without a parable spake He not unto them" (v. 33). And the second is written in the twelfth chapter of the same Gospel where we read: "And the common people heard Him gladly." (V. 37)

There can be no doubt that for most of us, common people that we are, there is something intriguing about a parable. There is something that arrests our attention, holds our interest, and (at least in the parables which have come to us from the lips of our divine Lord) something that gives us a vivid insight into sacred truth which, in many cases, could have come to us in no other way.

That is why the Savior again and again reduced the profound abstractions of His message to a simple narrative. He clothed His thoughts, as it were, in flesh and blood and made them visual. To explain God's attitude toward His lost and straying children, for instance, He delivered no formal theological dissertation, but He told three short stories in quick succession: the stories of the lost sheep, the lost coin, and the lost son (Luke 15).

Indeed, anyone who reads the four Gospels is bound to remember the Master Teacher and Master Evangelist as the *Master Storyteller.* "Without a story spake He not unto them . . . and the common people heard Him gladly."

It is this approach which the author has sought to follow in the devotional readings here presented. He makes no claim to originality for all of the illustrations used. Many have been culled from his reading. For these he wishes to give credit to their original authors. Others have been adapted or modified to suit his specific purpose. Others are original, being based on personal observation or personal experience. All have been published serially in the Christian family magazine *This Day.*

A topical index in the back of this volume will help the reader select devotional readings best suited to his specific needs and circumstances. This index will also help the layman, Sunday school teacher, or clergyman who is in search of an apt illustration for his public address. It is the author's prayer that, as the reader journeys through these pages, he will gain fresh insights into the marvelous love of God as it has been revealed to us in Jesus Christ His Son.

THE AUTHOR

Contents

My Hand in His

My Hand in His

A traveler in the Scottish highlands saw a cluster of beautiful flowers far down the mountainside. He promised a reward to a shepherd boy if he would pick them, offering to let him down by a rope.

The boy eyed the stranger suspiciously and then, without a word, disappeared into the woods. In a moment he was back, but with him was his father. He was willing to be let down the mountainside *provided the rope was in his father's hands!*

Our Father in heaven permits our feet to come upon steep and slippery places, far down the mountainside of human suffering; but no matter how deep the valley or how difficult the descent, we can always rest secure in the conviction that our times are in His hands. He holds the rope!

We shall go just so far down the hillside of adversity as His *love* would have us go. He knows our strength, and He knows our weakness.

He knows even before we go down into the valley what flowers we are to bring back with us — what lesson in humility, what lesson in trust, what lesson in Christian virtue — and He will bring us up again as soon as we have gathered the flowers for which His love has sent us.

If ever there was a man who knew what it meant to descend from the mountaintop of prosperity and good fortune down into the abyss of bitter disappointment, that man was David — the man "after God's own heart."

Small wonder that David on one occasion, when he felt the ground crumbling beneath his feet, cast a pleading eye heavenward and exclaimed: "My times are in Thy hand." (Ps. 31:15)

Thus it has been with all believers of all time. Thus it can be for you and me. Through faith in God's unchanging promises, particularly through faith in the Gospel of salvation through His beloved Son, I can place my hand into the hand of God and know that He will never let me go.

What a comfort, when my cross seems heaviest, when it seems that my life has neither plan nor purpose, when it seems that I am being pushed about by a blind and merciless fate, to remember that in every valley of affliction — my hand is in His. And with my hand in His, I am forever safe. His omnipotent hand will hold me. His affectionate hand will guide me.

> I am trusting Thee, Lord Jesus;
> Never let me fall.
> I am trusting Thee forever —
> And for all.

He Loved Me!

$\mathbf{F}$our-year-old Mary Ann sat in her accustomed church pew, closely snuggled to her mother's side. The organ was playing the prelude, and little Mary Ann's eyes were intent on the picture of Jesus on the front of her Sunday school leaflet.

Finally, looking up into her mother's face, and pointing to the picture of the Savior, she whispered with a joy that lit up her features: *"He loved me!"*

Yes, Mary Ann, He loved you! If only we who are older could always remember, with joy and gratitude, the love which He had in His heart for all of us! If only we could repeat, with the same fervency and the same affection, those simple words of the apostle Paul: "He loved me and gave Himself for me." (Gal. 2:20)

All that we need to know for time and for eternity is summed up in the simple sweetness of those tender words. Does the world hate me? He *loved* me! Do I find the way hard, the path dark, the night lonely, the world friendless? He *loved* me! Does the shadow of tomorrow's burden haunt my every step and cause my feet to falter? He *loved* me — and His love can never change. His love is everlasting.

Or is it my sins that seek to cause my heart alarm? My crimson record? My restless conscience? I need not fear. *"He gave Himself for me!"* He took my sins to Calvary's cross and drowned them in the depths of His

[5]

unending love. He bore my guilt. He paid my debt. He endured my punishment. He suffered all — He gave *Himself* for me!

What a blessed, soul-reviving thought to inscribe across the threshold of each new day! Tomorrow morning, *every* morning, every hour of the day and every day of the week, our hearts can be filled with the glad assurance: My Savior loves me! He gave Himself for me!

Just as little Mary Ann looked up into the face of her mother, we can lift grateful hearts heavenward and exclaim:

> Oh, the height of Jesus' love!
> Higher than the heavens above,
> Deeper than the depths of sea,
> Lasting as eternity;
> Love that found me — wondrous thought! —
> Found me when I sought Him not.

The Sense of Sin

A Christian young lady came to her pastor with a perplexing problem. She had been regular in her church attendance, conscientious in her daily prayers, and consistent in her attendance at the Lord's Supper; and yet she had been unable to rid herself of a haunting sense of sin.

"Why is it," she asked, "that my girl friends who never go to church, and who freely admit that they have never taken religion seriously, are never troubled by any consciousness of guilt?"

Her problem was not a new one to the pastor. "Tell me," he said, "if I were to lay a hundred pounds of steel upon a corpse, would it feel the load?"

"No. I'm sure it wouldn't."

"Why not?"

"Because the corpse has no life in it and is unable to *feel* the weight."

"Exactly!" replied the pastor. "And that is why the person who is still indifferent to his spiritual needs can say that he doesn't feel the weight of sin. He's dead — spiritually."

It has always been true that the Christian has been more conscious of his personal unworthiness in the sight of God — his personal *sinfulness* — than the careless unbeliever.

David, the man of God, had to admit: "I acknowledge my transgressions, and my sin is ever before me" (Ps. 51:3). The apostle Paul, whom God used mightily for the spread of the Christian Gospel, had to lament: "I know that in me . . . there dwelleth no good thing. . . . Oh, wretched man that I am!" (Rom. 7:18-24)

There is really nothing surprising in the Christian's consciousness of sin. The man who walks in darkness is unconscious of the smudges on his body; but let him walk out into the light, and he immediately becomes conscious of his dirty hands.

The Christian walks in light! And the closer he draws to "the Light of Life," the more conscious he becomes of his soiled garments.

Nor is there anything surprising in the Christian's *sensitiveness* to his personal guilt. He has seen his sin in terms of Calvary. It was a sensitive heart, a Christian heart, that wrote:

> Ye who think of sin but lightly,
> Nor suppose the evil great,
> Here may view its nature rightly,
> Here its guilt may estimate.

No, there was nothing surprising at all in this young lady's concern over her personal sin. In fact, her deep concern was a sign that the Spirit of God was indeed working in her heart.

And yet she had no reason to worry. For the same Bible that told her that she was a sinner in God's sight also tells her: "If our heart condemn us, God is greater than our heart and knoweth all things." (1 John 3:20)

God, who is greater than our heart, looks at us, not in our sins, but in Christ. And in Christ there is abundant pardon and mercy. As the apostle Paul assures us: "There is therefore now no condemnation to them which are in Christ Jesus." (Rom. 8:1)

Sinners? Yes. But *forgiven* sinners. Forgiven through Christ.

The Secret of the Open Door

It happened many years ago, on a cool October morning in a seaside village in England. A pastor was visiting in a cobbler's shop, watching him pound the leather with his hammer, and listening as the happy cobbler hummed a merry tune.

Looking around the dingy little shop, with its cramped quarters and its crowded shelves, the pastor marveled that the man before him never seemed depressed.

"Man," he finally said, "don't you *ever* get tired of this narrow life — the same thing day after day in this crowded little room?"

The cobbler walked to a back door, opened it wide, and said: "Whenever I start feeling depressed, Pastor, I just open this door."

As the door swung open, the room was flooded with a new glory. Within the twinkling of an eye the cramped little shop had been glorified by the vastness of its new relationship — to the fields and skies and rolling sea, and to the Creator of them all.

In a sense, it is very much the same with life in general. All of us are in danger of living within the closed doors of our immediate circumstances, looking at the same dark walls day after day, the walls of our gloomy thoughts, walls which we have placarded with our own "insuperable" problems.

How different, when we *open* the door — and link our little lives to God's eternal purposes, to the whole panorama of His love and beauty as revealed in Jesus Christ, our Savior! How different when the fresh air and sunlight of eternity are permitted to flood into the dark and dingy cubicles of time!

Do our problems look too big for us today? Are the walls of life, as it were, closing in on us — crushing out all faith and joy and hope? Open the door! Look out — look up — look into the vastness of God's love, as He Himself reveals it!

On the far horizon we see those words of imperishable assurance: "If God be for us, who can be against us? He that spared not His own Son, but delivered Him up for us all, how shall He not with Him also freely give us *all* things?" (Rom. 8:31,32) including the inner joy our heart is seeking!

"Love That Found Me"

In the timber mountains of the Northwest a five-year-old was lost. Night came. The citizens and rangers searched frantically in every cave and on every mountainside.

Snow began to fall. Blanket upon blanket of gleaming white covered the floor of the forest, but no Bobby could be found.

The next morning the weary father, fatigued from an all-night search, kicked against what seemed to be a log in his path. But when the snow fell loose, a small boy stretched, yawned, sat up, and exclaimed: "O Daddy! I've found you at last!"

Now — *who* found *whom?*

Little Bobby in his excitement might say: "O Daddy, I've found you at last!" But the bleeding heart of the older man knew that it was he — and not Bobby — who had done the searching and the finding.

Men sometimes talk about finding God. Learnedly, they speak of the quest for God, the search for certainty, and the discovery of the divine.

But it was not God who was lost, it was *we!* Nor was it *we* who found *God,* it was *God* who found *us.* In that precious "lost and found" chapter of the Gospel according to Saint Luke (chapter 15) it was the sheep that was lost, and not the shepherd; the coin, and not the woman; the prodigal son, and not his father.

If we are members of Christ's church today, it is not because of any decision of our own. The decision was God's. He found us. He found us outside, and He brought us in.

If any man had a right to say that he had "found God," surely Martin Luther might have said so. But what did he say? "I believe that I cannot by my own reason or strength believe in Jesus Christ, my Lord, or come to Him. But the Holy Ghost has *called* me by the Gospel." Luther did not find God. God found Martin Luther and by the power of His Spirit, working through His Word, made Martin Luther an heir of heaven.

Today, as we contemplate the wonders of God's love as revealed in the Gospel of salvation, we thank Him for having gone out into the night and having brought us into the warmth and light which are ours in our most holy faith.

If today we are safe in the Shepherd's keeping, it is only because God from eternity saw us out in the darkness of sin and decreed that we should be brought into the shelter of His fold.

The entire distance between God and man was covered by God!

Today we are not lost, simply because God found us! "Herein is love," says John, "not that *we* loved *God,* but that *He* loved *us*" (1 John 4:10). That was the marvelous thought that prompted the poet to exclaim:

> Love that found me — wondrous thought! —
> Found me when I sought Him not.

Just a Day at a Time

(Thoughts at the turn of the year)

An anxious patient, lying on her sickbed, turned to her doctor and asked: "Doctor, how long shall I have to lie here and suffer?"

"Just a day at a time," replied the kind and wise physician.

Just a day at a time! What a wonderful philosophy of life — especially at this season of the year when we turn the pages of our crisp new calendars and scan the 365 bright numerals, into each of which, God willing, we shall pour twenty-four hours of living.

Just a day at a time the new year will come to us with its new burdens, its new duties, its hopes, and its fears. Thank God, we do not have to live all of the new year at once; it comes only a day at a time. Even tomorrow is never ours until it becomes today.

It is a blessed secret, this living just a day at a time. Anyone who has seen the crushing burden of his sin lifted by Calvary's cross can carry his own little burden, however heavy, until nightfall. Anyone who knows that his Savior has completed the tremendous work of his redemption can do his *own* work, however hard, just for a day. Anyone who has beheld the patience of his Lord and Savior can live patiently, lovingly, helpfully — until the sun goes down.

[14]

God gives us night to shut down the curtain of darkness on our little days. We cannot see beyond, nor do we need to. Tomorrow is in His hand — He is asking us only to live today.

And so, as we stand upon the threshold of a brand-new year, a year which, if it continues the pace of the year just past, will record great changes in the history of our country and in the history of us as families and as individuals, let us not be frightened by the overwhelming greatness of its possibilities, but let us rather find comfort and strength in the fact that God has cut the coming year into smaller pieces, and we shall have to live it "just a day at a time."

And He has promised us that as our days, so shall our strength be (Deut. 33:25). We have God's own assurance that each day throughout the coming year, yes, each day throughout *all* coming years, will find us equipped with that amount of strength that will be necessary to bear its burden, to endure its trial, and to fight its battle through.

Let us, then, not try to live February in January. Let us not try to live tomorrow today. Above all, let us not *fear* the prospect of the unknown future. God, the All-Wise, the Almighty, and the Eternal — with whom there are no yesterdays and with whom there are no tomorrows — has gone ahead, and when we reach our own tomorrow, we shall find Him there.

> Lord, for tomorrow and its needs
> I do not pray;
> Keep me, my God, from stain of sin
> Just for today.

Let me both diligently work
And duly pray;
Let me be kind in word and deed
Just for today.

Let me in season, Lord, be grave,
In season gay;
Let me be faithful to Thy grace
Just for today.

"Shut Out" and "Shut In"

(Lenten Thoughts)

Mr. Brown had just stepped from a crowded drugstore into a telephone booth. He had been told that an urgent message awaited him at home.

But try as hard as he would, he could not distinguish the voice at the other end of the line — and the message was lost in the clatter and the clamor of the crowded store.

Finally he managed to catch one sentence. "John, dear," said the voice in the telephone, "please close the door behind you." He had forgotten to close the door to the booth, and the noises of the drugstore had drowned out the distant voice from home.

As we prepare to step from the busy, noisy world into the hush and quiet of our Lenten season, we have every reason to make sure that we have closed the doors behind us. We dare not run the risk of missing the "still, small voice" which speaks to the Christian heart through the contemplation of the suffering Savior.

There are some things which we shall have to shut *out,* and there are some things which we shall have to shut *in,* if we wish to make the coming season a period of spiritual refreshment.

[17]

Ours is a busy, noisy world. And we are not referring now primarily to the throbbing world of manufacture, trade, and commerce. We are referring to the busy world which has broken into the midst of the average family circle.

Twelve-year-old Johnnie with his after-school basketball practice and after-supper homework, 18-year-old Margie with her high school functions and social obligations, dad with his evening meetings, and mother with her multiplying away-from-home interests added to her many household duties, the family radio with its blaring "first five" every evening, and the television set with its daily fare of entertainment and excitement — all combine to give us a picture which very much resembles the noisy drugstore, against which Mr. Brown had forgotten to shut the door.

We shall have to face the facts honestly: If we are to hear the "still, small voice" of the Lenten season within our family circle, we shall have to shut some things *out* that have assumed places of importance in our daily family living.

And we shall have to shut some things *in*. Have we grown remiss in our daily prayer life — our personal, private prayers? Then let us find time during the coming weeks to shut ourselves in with God for daily spiritual communion.

Have we permitted family worship to be crowded out of our regular daily routine?

There is a message in the Lenten season, a message from the Father's heart to ours; a message of peace and pardon, of courage and strength, of life and hope, through the wounds and death of Jesus Christ, our Savior.

As another Ash Wednesday approaches, let us ask ourselves: Have we closed the doors — against the intrusions of a busy world that would rob us of that message?

Easter Triumph

There is a story that when the battle of Waterloo was being fought, the people of England were dependent upon a system of semaphore signals to learn of the tide of battle. One of these signals was on the tower of Winchester Cathedral.

Late in the day it flashed the signal: "Wellington defeated!" Just at that moment one of those sudden English clouds of fog obscured the signal. The news of disaster spread throughout the city. The whole countryside was steeped in dark despair.

Suddenly the fog lifted, and the remainder of the message could be read. There were not only *two* words being flashed. There were *four*. And the completed message read: "Wellington defeated — the enemy!" In a moment, sorrow was turned into joy, defeat into victory.

So it was when Jesus was laid into the tomb on that first Good Friday. Hope had died even in the hearts of His most loyal friends. After the frightful crucifixion the fog of disappointment and disillusionment had settled on the faithful few. They had read only part of the divine message. "Christ defeated!" was all they knew.

But on the third day the impenetrable fog of despair lifted, and there was flashed to the world the completed message, not of defeat, but of victory, not of death, but of life. For the completed Easter message was a triumphant shout: *Christ defeated death!*

Good Friday and Easter are inseparables in God's great plan of man's redemption. St. Paul wrote to his Christians at Rome that Christ "was delivered for our offenses and was raised again for our justification." (Rom. 4:25)

On Good Friday the Savior was offered up as the atoning Sacrifice for the sins of all men ("delivered for our offenses"); but on Easter morning the heavenly Father raised His Son in order to proclaim to all men everywhere that He had accepted the payment of His Son for the world's iniquity ("raised again for our justification").

Easter, therefore, is pre-eminently a day of triumph. It is the day on which the Son of God emerged victorious over sin, death, hell, and the grave.

> He lives triumphant from the grave,
> He lives eternally to save,
> He lives all-glorious in the sky,
> He lives exalted there on high.
>
> He lives, all glory to His name!
> He lives, my Jesus, still the same.
> Oh, the sweet joy this sentence gives,
> "I know that my Redeemer lives!"

Greater Than Our Heart

There are moments in our lives when we look into the secret chambers of our heart for evidence that we are God's children — and we *fail* to find that evidence!

Searching our souls for assurance of our salvation, we find assurance only of our sin. Our very heart condemns us, accuses us of innumerable transgressions, and finally confronts us with the crushing judgment: you are not a Christian!

It is at moments like these that the divine assurance of a memorable statement of St. John falls like sweetest music on our soul. "If our heart condemn us," he says, "God is greater than our heart and knoweth all things." (1 John 3:20)

Though our heart condemn us a thousand times, though its inner precincts roar and thunder endless accusations, "God is greater than our heart and knoweth all things."

To anyone but a Christian it is a terrible thought to realize that God "knoweth all things." For among those "things" which must be a part of His knowledge are the unnumbered sins which lurk within the human heart, like skeletons in a closet, and which the unforgiven sinner seeks desperately to hide from the all-seeing eye of an all-knowing God.

And yet to the Christian there is comfort in the fact that God "knoweth all things." Why? What is it that God knows — that can reverse the terrible judgment of our heart? What is it that God knows — that our deceitful heart has failed to tell us?

Ah, right there is the difference between the Christian faith and all the religions which men have devised. God looks at us through *Christ!* He knows, to be sure, that we are sinners; but He also knows that in Christ our guilt has been atoned, that in Christ our sins have been washed away. He knows that in Christ our sin-stained lives have been accounted righteous in His sight.

God *knows* these things, and there is never a moment when He does *not* know them. Our heart may forget — but God knows. Just as a heavy storm cloud may blot out the sun for a moment and enshroud our little world in total darkness but can never remove the sun from the skies, so our little moments of doubt and despair can never erase the sun of God's mercy from the firmament of His promises.

Our heart, forgetful of His mercy, may confront us with the claims of God's consuming justice. But God, ever mindful of His Son's atonement, confronts us with the sweet assurance: "My son, My daughter, be of good cheer; thy sins are forgiven thee." (Matt. 9:2)

Therefore, let heart, soul, mind or whatever other faculty I may have, tell me that I am *lost.* It matters not! My source of assurance rests in His all-knowing love. The anchor of my soul has found its hold in the eternal Rock of Ages. He is "greater than my heart." He knows all things. And HE tells me I am saved.

The Beauty Is Inside

It was a hot summer day. Two high school girls had spent most of their Sunday afternoon in a leisurely stroll through the downtown section of the city. Suddenly they found themselves directly in front of a huge cathedral.

Looking at the lofty stained-glass window, which their art teacher had told them to be sure to see, one of the girls stopped short and grunted: "Nothing beautiful in that! Just a lot of dirty glass."

A little old lady, overhearing the remark, walked up to the girls and said: "You can't judge the beauty of an art-glass window from the outside. Why don't you step inside?"

The girls went in — and, before they knew it, they were standing motionless and enthralled, their faces bathed in a symphony of color which was pouring from the stained-glass window. The little old lady was right: you just can't judge a stained-glass window from the outside.

The same is true of the Bible. If you really want to know if the Bible is God's Word, there is only one way to find out, and that is to "go inside." All the fine arguments, all the logical "proofs," all the compelling evidence based on historical study will not mean nearly as much as a reverent reading of the Book itself.

The strongest evidence that the Bible has been given to us by God is one which cannot be passed from one man to another. It is a conviction which the Holy Spirit pours into the hearts of those who "go inside" — of those who read the Book and place themselves under its converting influence.

There are, of course, other evidences of the Bible's divine authorship. In more than 2,000 instances the Bible identifies itself as the Word of God. Again and again its prophecies have been fulfilled. Jesus Himself placed His stamp of divine approval on the Scriptures. Wherever the Bible has gone, it has left a trail of blessing. Nowhere else in all the world could men have found a way of escape from sin and hell such as God has given them in one simple Bible verse: *John 3:16.*

These are all valid ways of "proving" that the Bible is God's Word. But, like our high school girls to whom we referred above, it is possible to discuss all these "proofs" while standing on the outside of the Book — and thus miss the greatest proof of all, the witness of the Holy Spirit through the power of the Word itself.

The apostle Peter tells us that we are born again not by arguments *about* the Bible, but "by the Word of God, which liveth and abideth forever, . . . and this is the Word which by the Gospel is preached unto you." (1 Peter 1:23-25)

The best advice to the honest inquirer about the Bible is to *go inside.* That is where its beauty lies.

In the Upper Branches

An elderly woman had been confined to her bedroom for several years. Each spring she watched from her window as the same robin returned and built its nest *high* in a nearby tree.

One morning she called to her daughter and said nervously: "Look! Our robin is building her nest in one of the *lower* branches this year. I'm afraid the neighbor's cat can reach it."

A few days later she looked out of her window — to find the ground beneath that branch covered with feathers. The neighbor's cat had indeed found the lower branch within its reach — and the robin was dead!

As Christians we, too, have the choice of building our lives in the "upper branches" or in the "lower" — of living thrillingly close to God or dangerously close to the world. We have the choice of filling our minds with thoughts of goodness, love, and lofty aspiration or filling our minds with the mean and the low and the trivial.

We are living in the *lower* branches, for instance, when we cultivate a taste for books and magazines which pander to the lower passions, when we frequent places of amusement which cater to the lusts of the flesh, when we associate with friends and companions of whom we know that they delight in flouting the requirements of purity and decency.

[26]

How many a young person who has built his life in these lower branches has been snatched, almost unawares, by the Tempter and hurled to his destruction!

We are living in the *upper* branches, removed farthest from the Tempter's wiles, when we live in daily communion with our Savior, when we occupy ourselves diligently with His work, when we take an active part in church activities, when we associate with Christian friends, and when we make a deliberate effort to fill our minds with those thoughts only which we could lay bare in the presence of the Master.

That is what the apostle had in mind when he said: "Whatsoever things are true, whatsoever things are honest, whatsoever things are just, whatsoever things are pure, whatsoever things are lovely, whatsoever things are of good report; if there be any virtue, and if there be any praise, think on these things." (Phil. 4:8)

The man who fills his mind with "these things" is living in the upper branches, and the crafty enemy of his soul will not find him an easy prey. Of those who have "set their affections on things above," the apostle says that their life "is hid with Christ in God." (Col. 3:3)

Scripture admonishes us to "walk in the Spirit," that is, live on the level of the things of God; and then it adds the promise: "and ye shall not fulfill the lusts of the flesh." (Gal. 5:16)

On what level has our life been moving — on the upper or on the lower? Have we built our nest in the upper or in the lower branches?

When Disappointment Comes

We are told that in the Botanical Gardens at Oxford, England, a fine pomegranate was cut down almost to the root because it bore nothing but leaves.

Some time later the keeper was able to report that a marvelous transformation had taken place and that the tree was now bearing fruit in abundance. All that it had needed was to be "cut back" — and to be "cut back" severely.

Our heavenly Father sometimes finds it necessary to "cut back" the trees that are growing in *His* garden. We Christians are those trees — planted, cultivated, and nurtured by a miracle of His grace.

Of us the Bible says: "Every branch that beareth fruit, He purgeth it (that is, He prunes it) that it may bring forth *more* fruit" (John 15:2). Notice! This pruning is done on the branches that are bearing fruit — that they may bring forth *more* fruit. The brittle brush and useless twigs must constantly be cut away to assure and to multiply the yield.

Sometimes we wonder why it is that devout and pious Christians, men and women who strive with all their hearts to conform their lives to the will of Christ, must suffer one disappointment after another. Why must the righteous suffer bitter visitations at the hands of a merciful Father?

[28]

The complete answer to that question will never be given this side of heaven. But God has revealed just enough of His design for us to pin our faith to. "Every branch that beareth fruit, He purgeth it that it may bring forth *more* fruit." We are to be the better, the more fruitful — for our "cutback."

If ever there was a man who had to undergo frequent prunings, it was the apostle Paul. In 2 Corinthians 11: 24-33 he lays his breast bare, as it were, and displays the countless scars of the pruning hook of God's unsearchable providence. "Beaten with rods . . . stoned . . . in perils in the sea . . . in hunger and thirst . . . in cold and nakedness." And yet no one will deny that the life of this great man of God was more fruitful because of these painful visitations.

And so it is with us and with everyone who has come to God through faith in Christ. Has our heavenly Father perhaps found it necessary to "cut back" drastically some branch in our life on which we had pinned our highest hopes? Have we experienced such a "cutback" through the loss of health? the loss of wealth? the loss of a beloved son or daughter? Have we had to taste the bitter ashes of utter disillusionment?

These are painful "cutbacks," to be sure. But they are "cutbacks" with a gracious purpose. Let us always remember, when the days of pruning come, that God is not cutting down the tree — He is rather improving one of its branches.

Could His love send us any sorrow which, in His wisdom, was not intended for our joy?

Remember Whose Child You Are

The story is told of a boy who was leaving home for college. His father had included him in the morning prayer at the breakfast table, asking God to protect him and to grant him success in the career which he was undertaking.

Rising from the table, the young man expected to receive some final bit of advice and instruction from his father. But he was surprised when, after a moment's silence, the older man merely placed his hand on his shoulder, looked at him kindly, and said: "My boy, remember whose son you are!"

Need he have said any more than that?

We Christians, too, are children of a Father — temporarily away from our Father's house. "Behold, what manner of love the Father hath bestowed upon us that we should be called the sons of God!" (1 John 3:1) exclaims the apostle John. Yes, sons and daughters of God — through Christ!

In his letters to us, the Holy Scriptures, how often has our heavenly Father admonished us to remember whose children we are! "Ye were sometimes darkness," He writes to the Ephesians and to us, "but now are ye light in the Lord; walk as children of light." (Eph. 5:8)

And the Savior Himself has told us: "Let your light so shine before men that they may see your good works and glorify your *Father* which is in heaven." (Matt. 5:16)

How have we been behaving "away from home," away from our Father's house? Have we been reflecting credit upon our family name — *"children of God"?*

As a rule, men are extremely careful to protect the good name of their family. The Smith children are eager to protect the good name of the Smith parents, and the Smith parents are eager to protect the good name of the Smith children. A deep sense of family loyalty and family pride makes them want to do those things only which will reflect credit upon the name of Smith.

In the measure in which we remember from day to day — in our home, in our shop, and at our play — that we are "the children of God," in that measure we shall seek to reflect credit upon the name of Him whom we call "Father."

If we are the children of God by faith in Christ, it is inevitable that we shall share in some of the family traits which are common to all His children — love, mercy, forbearance, righteousness, honesty, faithfulness.

Just as the children of earthly parents frequently "take after their father," so those who have come to faith in Christ Jesus are expected to "take after" their heavenly Father. From day to day, through the power of His Holy Spirit, they are to become more and more like Him — more loving, more patient, more kindly, more honest, more truthful, more righteous.

Yes, it will pay us to — remember whose children we are!

[31]

Give God Your Life

The evangelist Moody was conducting services in a town in England. Upon returning to his friend's home in the evening, the friend inquired: "Well, how many were converted tonight?"

"Two and a half," Moody replied. "Why, what do you mean?" asked the friend. "Was it two adults and a child?" "No," replied the evangelist, "it was two children and an adult. The children have given their lives to Christ in their youth, while the adult has come with only the fraction of his that is left."

While it is true that the angels of heaven rejoice over *"every* sinner that repenteth" — no matter how young or how old — it is also true, as Moody pointed out so graphically, that the man who comes to faith in later years is giving the Lord a proportionately smaller fraction of his life.

How much of *our* life are we giving to the Lord? The question is not how much of our time, how much of our talents, or how much of our money we have placed at His disposal; but how much of our life? Of the Macedonians we read that before they gave anything to the Lord, they "first gave their *own selves*." (2 Cor. 8:5)

Have we surrendered ourselves to the Lord in that way? It's a comparatively simple matter to pry ourselves loose from a five-dollar bill or from an evening's entertainment and to give the five-dollar bill or the evening to the Lord. But it's an entirely different matter to pry ourselves loose from our *self* — and to put our *self* wholly at His disposal.

Yet that is what the Lord expects of us, and nothing less. Out of gratitude for His surpassing mercy, revealed to us and to all men on Calvary's cross, we are to subordinate our will to His. We are to surrender our self to Him.

We are to say with Paul: "I am crucified with Christ; nevertheless I live; yet not I, but Christ liveth in me; and the life which I now live in the flesh I live by the faith of the Son of God, who loved me and gave Himself for me." (Gal. 2:20)

Can we honestly say that? Can we honestly say that the life which we are living now is being lived "by the faith of the Son of God, who loved me and gave Himself for me"? Can we honestly say: "I live; yet not I, but Christ liveth in me"?

If not, we have not yet given our life fully to God. We may have given Him some of our money, some of our time, some of our talents; but we have not yet given Him our life.

Take my life and let it be consecrated, Lord, to Thee.

The Clocks of Heaven

Travelers to distant countries have been known to keep one timepiece set to the time of their native land so that — for reasons of sentiment — they might always know what time it is in the homeland.

In a somewhat similar sense the Christian pilgrim keeps one clock, the clock of his faith and trust, in time with the clocks in his Father's house above. There is a measurement of time which is known only to the believing and trusting heart — a measurement which is divided not into days and hours and minutes, but into the constantly repeated assurances of God's eternal promises.

The answer to my prayer, the lifting of my cross, the deliverance from a long-felt sorrow, or the granting of a long-sought pleasure — are all scheduled for fulfillment, not according to the clocks and calendars on my kitchen wall, but according to the clocks of eternity, which are "telling time" on the walls of my Father's house.

God never comes too late with too little or too soon with too much. He is always on time — His time. His delays, when delays occur, are always the delays of love. His "little whiles" (John 16:19) are always the preludes to greater revelations of His mercy.

For young Joseph, thrown into the pit by his jealous brothers or later cast into prison by angry Potiphar, it may have seemed that the clocks of heaven had stopped. It may have seemed that the promises of God were empty, vain, and futile. But he lived to see the day when all the clocks of heaven struck the hour of God's fulfillment. (Gen. 50:20)

Our heavenly Father assures us: "For a small moment have I forsaken thee, but with great mercies will I gather thee" (Is. 54:7). And again: "Weeping may endure for a night, but joy cometh in the morning." (Ps. 30:5)

What a comfort to know that because of the life and death and resurrection of our beloved Savior, all the clocks of heaven have been set for our eternal welfare! With David we can say in confident assurance: "My times are in Thy hand" (Ps. 31:15), for we know that our times are in the hands of Him who loved us and gave Himself for us.

It is true that even for the best of Christians there are times when it seems that the clocks of heaven are running slow. There are times indeed when the purposes of God seem "past finding out," but in *Christ* we know that they are always the purposes of love.

Ashamed of Being a Christian

The story is told of a Christian young man who went to spend several months in a Canadian lumber camp. The camp was notorious for its rough and lawless characters.

When the young man returned to his home town a few months later, one of his friends asked him how he had fared in that kind of company.

"Oh, fine," he said, "they never caught on that I was different!"

Several months in the company of godless men — and they had never "caught on" to the fact that he was a Christian! What a perfect record — *of shameful denial!* He had been afraid to admit, in the company of godless men, that he was a Christian, because he wasn't ready to bear the consequences.

But before we censure him too strongly, or before we begin to stroke ourselves in self-righteous satisfaction, let us ask ourselves: What has been our *own* record in the company of Christ's enemies?

Has it *really* been much better?

What hiding of our colors, what dodging of the issue, what shaving of the truth, what trimming of our sails, what flagrant, base denial of the Savior has our record often shown?

Of John the Baptist we read: "He confessed and denied not" (John 1:20). All too often we have "denied and confessed not."

The Christian high school boy (or girl) who for the first time finds himself associating with a "fast set," the Christian college coed who finds herself in company where foul lips are flouting the fundamental requirements of decency and purity, the Christian businessman who suddenly finds himself in the midst of blatant scoffers — how often do they find the strength and courage to stand up for Christ and to demonstrate their loyalty to Him?

Isn't it true that often they manage to hide their colors — uncomfortably perhaps, but successfully nevertheless — and later breathe a sigh of relief if their godless companions never "caught on" to the fact that they belonged to Christ?

There are glorious exceptions, it is true. But why should the precious name of Christ be denied so *often?*

Surely, each of us has reason to ask God to forgive us our sins of cowardice. And then, like Simon Peter, after he had been forgiven and restored by the Lord whom he had shamefully denied, we have reason to pray for courage to confess our Savior before friend and foe alike.

Ashamed of Jesus, that dear Friend
On whom my hopes of heaven depend?
No; when I blush, be this my shame,
That I no more revere His name!

The Fire on the Altar

A group of engineers, working for the Tennessee Valley Authority, came to the humble cottage of an elderly man. The purpose of their visit was to persuade him to vacate the place in which he was living — to make way for the tremendous TVA engineering project.

The old man was kind but firm. He had made up his mind to stay in the home where his father had lived and his grandfather before him. The engineers told him they would build him a new house to take the place of the dilapidated shack to which he had become so attached.

"But," insisted the friendly old man, "you don't understand. When my father was ready to leave this old world, he called me to his bedside and told me that this house had been built by his forefathers and that the fire started in this fireplace had never been permitted to go out. And my father made me promise, before he died, that I would never let this fire go out. I could never think of going back on my word."

It was not until the engineers had assured him that they would build him a new house and would carry some of the fire from the old fireplace to the new one, that the old man finally consented to have his home wrecked.

If only we *all* were as eager to keep the altar fires

burning in our hearts and in our homes as this old gentleman was to keep the fire burning in that fireplace!

The flame of Christian faith, of love and devotion, which burned brightly in the hearts of our parents (and their parents before them) — is it still burning just as brightly in our hearts and lives today? The fire on the family altar, the daily habit of family prayer, the frequent recourse to the familiar family Bible, the daily expression of a common family faith — is that fire still burning brightly?

Or has it long since flickered, sputtered, and finally succumbed to the winds of indifference, preoccupation, doubt, and disbelief? Alas, many a fire upon the altar which was enkindled by Christian parents has been permitted to languish and die upon the unused altars of their children!

The fire upon the altars of our hearts and homes must be rekindled every day. Let us pray God for a living family faith — a faith in Jesus Christ as Savior and as our familiar family Friend.

> Blest such a house, it prospers well,
> In peace and joy the parents dwell,
> And in their children's lot is shown
> How richly God can bless His own.

Strength for the "Inward Man"

When John Quincy Adams was a very old man, he was met one day by a friend who greeted him with the familiar words: "How do you do, Mr. Adams?"

The elderly gentleman replied: "John Quincy Adams himself is very well, thank you, but the house in which he lives is falling to pieces. Time and the seasons have nearly destroyed it. I think John Quincy Adams will soon have to move out. But he himself is very well, sir."

Mr. Adams was referring, of course, to his aging body, from which the passing years had taken their toll and from which his immortal soul would soon have to take its leave.

The apostle Paul put it another way: "Though our outward man perish, yet the *inward* man is renewed day by day." (2 Cor. 4:16)

For the child of God there is no dread in the rapid flight of time. The passing years may bring with them their multiplied reminders that "swift to its close ebbs out life's little day" — the waning strength, the fading vigor, the slowing step, the blurring vision — but they also bring with them the glorious assurances by which our "inward man" is renewed day after day.

How avidly the "inward man" of the maturing Christian feeds upon the precious Gospel promises! With each passing year these promises mean more and more to him. With each passing year they pour new strength, new courage, new joy, new hope into his soul.

How *could* it be otherwise? If God's promises are true (and in Christ all His promises are Yea and Amen), then every passing year brings us that much closer to the complete fulfillment of *all* His promises to us.

He who fulfilled His ancient pledges by the miracles of Bethlehem, of Calvary, and Joseph's Garden, will surely keep His promise to come again and take us to Himself. Each day of our earthly sojourn that we put behind us is, therefore, another day that we have traveled closer to our Father's house.

Small wonder that the believing child of God can say with the great apostle: "Though our outward man perish, yet the inward man is renewed day by day." For it is the inward man that is daily feeding on the refreshing manna of the promises of heaven.

> Here in the body pent,
> Absent from Him I roam,
> Yet nightly pitch my moving tent
> A day's march nearer home.

The Unfinished Sermon

Mr. Matthews was not much of a churchgoer. Like many men, he was content to carry his religion in his wife's name. That explained why on a certain Sunday morning he was seated comfortably at home, while his wife was attending the Sunday morning service.

It was just before noon when a sudden rainstorm blew up from the south. As an obliging husband, Mr. Matthews put on his raincoat, reached for an umbrella, jumped into the family car, and drove to the church to meet his wife.

As he hurried up to the church door, he met an elderly woman who was just leaving. "Is the sermon over?" he asked. "No," the kind old lady replied, "the sermon's only *half* over. The pastor has *preached* it. Now I'm going home to *do* it."

In a sense, those are the two divisions of every God-pleasing sermon. In the first place, we should *hear*. And, in the second place, we should *do* — we should do something about what we have heard. Too many sermons end after the first part. They are really never finished. Or, to stay with the language of the good old lady, they are never — *done!*

The apostle James had something to say about people who were content to live on unfinished sermons. "If any be a hearer of the Word," he says, "and not a doer, he is like unto a man beholding his natural face in a glass. For he beholdeth himself and goeth his way, and straightway forgetteth what manner of man he was." (James 1:23, 24)

Looking into a mirror will never remove a blemish from our face, comb our hair, or adjust our clothing properly. The looking must be followed by doing. Listening to sermons Sunday after Sunday will never, in itself, feed the poor, relieve the needy, or bring the comfort of the Gospel to others. There must be a resultant *doing*.

The plague of much of our church life today is the blight of the unfinished sermon — the sermon that was started by hearing but was never ended by doing.

Alas, that all too frequently the pastor's final "Amen" has been misunderstood to mean: "It is finished." In reality, it means: "It is true." And because the Word which we have heard is true, we can rely upon it, and we can go out and *act* upon it — *living* it from day to day.

Let us pray God that, by His grace, we may translate our hearing into fruitful Christian living!

"We Pray to Jesus"

The school nurse had just completed her health talk. There were still a few minutes for a brief review. "Tell me, Johnny," she said to a bright-eyed seven-year-old, "What is the first thing we do when we catch a cold?"

Johnny rose to his feet and replied in confident assurance: "We pray to Jesus!"

That wasn't the answer she expected. And for a moment she was at a loss for words. But only for a moment. For as she looked into the eager, open face of little Johnny, she looked into a soul that was filled with faith; and before she knew it, she heard herself replying: "Yes, Johnny, we pray to Jesus."

One thing the school nurse knew for sure — Johnny was from a Christian home. All the health talks in the world, as beneficial as they may be, could never mean as much to Johnny as the Christian faith he had learned at his mother's knee.

Does *your* child have that faith? Does he bring his big little problems to the Savior in prayer? Have you introduced him to the Friend of children? Have you done everything in your power to cultivate an intimate friendship between your child and Christ?

Jesus says: "Suffer the little children to come unto Me . . . of such is the kingdom of God" (Mark 10:14). Children who have been *brought* to Christ and *kept* with

[44]

Christ will *talk* to Christ—also about their childhood illnesses.

Our nation knows no starker tragedy than the fifteen to twenty million children in its midst who are growing up with no formal religious training of any kind. And the church itself can record few darker tragedies than the child in its midst who has only a nodding acquaintance with the Lord who bought him—who has never learned to walk with Him and to talk with Him.

What America needs today, above all else, is twenty million little Johnnies—children whose parents have brought them to their Savior, who have folded their little hands in prayer, who accompany them to church and Sunday school, and who by word and example are leading their children to ever higher planes of Christian life.

Borne by the Burden

A biologist tells how he watched an ant carrying a piece of straw which seemed almost too heavy for it to drag.

The ant came to a crack in the ground which was too wide for it to cross. It stood still for a time, as though perplexed by the situation, then put the straw across the crack and walked over on the straw.

If only we were as wise as that ant! We speak much about the burdens we must carry. But have we ever thought of converting our burdens into bridges, of having our burdens bear US up instead of our bearing THEM up?

The apostle Paul had learned the secret of being borne *up* by his burden instead of being borne *down* by it. Throughout his life he had been afflicted with a physical deformity or handicap, the exact nature of which we do not know.

But when he had once recognized his affliction as a part of God's good and gracious will for him, he exclaimed:

"Most gladly therefore will I rather glory in my infirmities that the power of Christ may rest upon me. . . . For when I am weak, then am I strong." (2 Cor. 12:9, 10)

If any man ever learned how to convert his burdens into bridges, that man surely was the apostle Paul. He took even his stripes and imprisonments and transformed them into open doors for the Gospel.

Every man who has found eternal life in the death of Jesus Christ, the Savior, can convert his burdens into bridges — bridges that lead from the darkness of despair into the brightness of assurance — bridges that lead from a purposeless and drab existence into a life of usefulness and beauty.

Some of the most cheerful and radiant personalities have been those whom God has visited with the greatest crosses. And those who have accomplished the greatest feats in the Kingdom have frequently been those who were borne to triumph upon the arms of a cross.

To know Christ is to know the love of God, and to know the love of God is to be assured of eternal fellowship with Him throughout the endless ages. In the light of that assurance no burden can continue to depress!

Have we learned to know the love of God in Christ? Have we experienced the assurance of His grace? Then He is saying to us, as once He said to Paul: "My grace is sufficient for thee, for My strength is made perfect in weakness." (2 Cor. 12:9)

And with His sustaining grace we shall be able to go on — converting all our burdens into bridges.

"Made in Heaven"

You've seen the familiar labels "Made in U. S. A.," "Made in Japan," "Made in Germany." But did you know that on every piece of bread you eat there is a label, invisible it is true, but nevertheless real, which says "Made in Heaven"?

Without the hand of God all the scientific knowledge and skill of men could not produce a single slice of bread. The formula, the ingredients, the various processes of nature which go to make our daily bread, are the property of heaven.

How fortunate for us that a benevolent God is willing to share with us those many priceless blessings — for the manufacture of which He still holds the patent!

Every spring the farmer sows his seed, and the city dweller who is fortunate enough to have a garden plants his lettuce, radishes, and garden vegetables.

We can prepare the soil — God's soil. We can sow the seed — God's seed. We can wait for the rain — God's rain. And we can count on the daily warmth of the sun — God's sun.

But without God's soil, God's seed, God's rain, and God's sun, who could create a single head of lettuce or produce a single grain from which to make the flour from which we make our bread?

Christ taught us to recognize God's creatorship and

ownership when He taught us to pray: "Give us this day our daily bread." (Matt. 6:11)

The Bible assumes our dependence on God for our daily food when it says: "The eyes of all wait upon Thee, and Thou givest them their meat in due season. Thou openest Thine hand and satisfiest the desire of every living thing." (Ps. 145:15, 16)

It is this recognition which leads Christian people to fold their hands before every meal and to offer thanks to Heaven. Recognizing the label of Heaven, they voice their gratitude to the Owner.

Having been restored to sonship with God through faith in Christ, they accept the gifts of Heaven as evidence of a Father's love. Christ has made them God's children, and as God's children they rejoice over every gift that comes from the Father's hand.

What a different place this world would be if we could all get our labels straight! The next time you sit down to a meal, trace several of the items on your menu back to their original sources — and see if everyone of them wasn't *made in heaven!*

Light and Shadow

Recently we flew from Los Angeles to St. Louis. We were about ten thousand feet up as we crossed a little valley just east of the Sierra Nevada Mountains.

As we looked up into endless space, everything was bright and azure blue. To the left and to the right everything was bathed in brilliant sunshine.

Some miles away, at a level somewhat lower than the plane, drifted a fleecy cloud which, from the top, looked like a downy angel pillow, fluffed, and snowy white — with an embroidered edge of gray.

Because the floating cloud was some miles to our left, we could also see the valley which lay beneath it. The valley was a patch of black, a land of shadow, shut off from the brilliant sun by the billowy cloud which spread above it.

As the cloud moved slowly southward, the north edge of the valley began to brighten; and we suppose that if we could have kept our point of vantage stationary, we would soon have seen the entire little valley emerge from the slowly moving shadow and be painted in bright and cheerful colors by the brilliant sun above.

As we looked out of our plane window, we couldn't help thinking how much that little valley reminded us of life. For a while its people saw nothing but the cloud above — for them *there was no sun.*

[50]

And yet we could see that the morning sun was shining brightly. As far as we could look — to the left, to the right, ahead, behind, or above — the sun had dispelled the early morning darkness. Only in that little valley did it seem that perhaps there was no sun.

And even there, the inevitable drift of the cloud was beginning to paint its northern slope with the brilliance of the sun above.

There are days in our lives when in our human shortsightedness we can see no evidence of God's sun of love above us, when all that we can see is the blackness of doubt, the shadow of uncertainty, the gloom of distressing foreboding. But that doesn't alter the fact that His sun of eternal love is fixed and sure.

The love of Him who sent His Son from heaven to earth that someday He might take you and me from earth to heaven — that love may be obscured from our human eyes for a season, but it is always there, more certain and more lasting than the rolling sun above.

Of one thing we can be forever certain: above the cloud that hangs above us the Sun of Grace is always shining.

Judge not the Lord by feeble sense,
But trust Him for His grace;
Behind a frowning providence
He hides a smiling face.

" . . . But Calvary Does"

A man who had misspent his life lay critically ill. Turning to his pastor, he asked: "Do you think that a deathbed repentance does away with a whole life of sin?" "No," the pastor answered quietly, "but *Calvary* does."

Calvary does away with every sin — the sins of our childhood, the sins of our youth, and those of our old age. "The blood of Jesus Christ, His Son, cleanseth us from *all* sin," says St. John (1 John 1:7). The Lord tells us through the prophet Isaiah: "Though your sins be as scarlet, they shall be as white as snow; though they be red like crimson, they shall be as wool" (Is. 1:18). And that means *all* of our sins!

It's not a question of being late or being early, of being more guilty or less guilty, of being very old or being very young — it's a question, rather, of accepting *now* the abundant pardon which is ours through the limitless love of Jesus Christ, our Savior.

There is love for all, there is mercy for all, and there is pardon for all alike.

Do you feel that you have been harboring some secret sin too long to be forgiven, that you have trampled upon God's grace too long to ask for pardon? Take heart! The Scripture tells us that where sin abounded, there did God's love much more abound. If you are still able to read these words, it is *not too late.* "Now is the accepted time. Now is the day of salvation." (2 Cor. 6:2)

The thief on the cross was late — *very* late — but not too late! The hour was late in the life of Zacchaeus, but not too late, for he still was privileged to hear from the lips of the Savior: *"This day* is salvation come to this house!" (Luke 19:9.) This day! Have you recognized this day as a day of grace?

> Today Thy mercy calls us
> To wash away our sin.
> However great our trespass,
> Whatever we have been,
> However long from mercy
> Our hearts have turned away,
> Thy precious blood can cleanse us
> And make us white today.

No, nothing that we can do can make up for a whole life of sin. But Christ can. And Calvary does!

His Eye Is on the Sparrow

The other evening, while raking the grass, we experienced that sudden start which seizes one when unexpectedly one comes across something which is dead. Among the grasscuttings beneath our rake we detected the body of a lifeless sparrow.

For the rest of the evening that sparrow was on our mind. Again and again we thought of the words of the Savior: "Are not two sparrows sold for a farthing? And one of them shall not fall on the ground without your Father." (Matt. 10:29)

Could it be, we mused, that the same God who guides the destinies of men and nations was concerned about that sparrow our rake had touched? Could it *really* be? Yes, it could be, it *must* be, for the Son of God Himself had said so.

And if that be true of sparrows, what shall we say of us? Sometimes, it is true, it seems that God has passed us by, that we are the one person in the world for whom He has failed to plan and for whom He has failed to make provision.

But our heavenly Father doesn't *want* us to feel that way. Again and again the Savior points to the hand of His Father in the individual lives of His Christians. "Your Father knoweth what things ye have need of," He says. He who holds the planets in the hollow of His hand also holds the sparrows. "Fear ye not therefore; ye are of more value than *many* sparrows." (Matt. 10:31)

Think for a moment of what God has *already* done for us! Today we are feeding upon the green pastures of His Word and are being led beside the still waters of His comforting assurances, only because God from eternity saw us out in the desert of sin and decreed that we should be brought into the shelter of His fold. We were lost and would have remained forever lost, had not His mercy found us.

But His mercy *did* find us! His love *did* bring us into the safety of the fold. And dare we doubt that He who went the bitter path of Calvary in order that He might seek and save His wandering sheep — dare we doubt that He will care for us and keep us *now* that He has gathered us among His own?

Surely, He whose eye is on the sparrow, and without whose permissive providence not even one of these shall fall upon the ground, surely *He* will not forget those for whom He bled and died.

> My soul to Thee alone,
> O Savior, I commend.
> Thou, Jesus, having loved Thine own,
> Wilt love me to the end.

The Solitary Rose

A traveler was staying at a small-town hotel. As he looked from his second-story window, he saw a gorgeous red rose blooming in a vacant lot next door. It was a single, solitary rose; but somehow it seemed to be all the more beautiful just because it stood alone.

As he walked by the vacant lot during the noon hour, he remembered the rose and decided that, if he could find it, he would pick it. But the lot was full of weeds, many of them taller than the rose, and from the sidewalk he couldn't see the beautiful bloom.

The next morning as he looked from his second-floor window, there was the same velvety rose, sparkling with diamonds of dew in the rays of the morning sun. From the vantage of his window he figured the exact position of the rose in this labyrinth of weeds and determined to go down and pick it.

Forcing his way through the thick brush and the almost impenetrable welter of weeds, he finally came to the thin perpendicular stem which held the fragile rose. How could this rose be growing *here?*

Carefully he traced the fragile stem down to the ground. But the stem did not end there. Laboriously he traced the stem as it stretched along the ground amid the weeds — until finally, some distance away, he found the stem firmly rooted in a cultivated patch of ground in the yard next door. It was *there* that it got its sustenance!

How very much like the child of God was that single, solitary rose! Frequently God places His Christians in the very midst of weed patches — in the very midst of godless men and women — not, indeed, to take on the appearance of the weeds, but to give forth the fragrance of the rose and to bloom with its refreshing beauty.

And the nourishment and strength which makes possible this beauty and this fragrance come from "the cultivated patch of ground next door" — the life that is "hid with Christ in God" (Col. 3:3), the life that is rooted firmly in the Savior.

He who said: "I am the Vine, ye are the branches" (John 15:5), is the secret Source of strength and beauty behind many a solitary rose in the weed patches of this world.

"He's My Brother!"

It was Christmas Eve — at dusk. As the pastor approached the parsonage, returning from an errand, he passed a twelve-year-old boy trudging through the snow, carrying his five-year-old brother on his back.

The older boy was puffing — as his audible breath became visible in the crisp, cold air of an early winter's night. It was evident that the burden on his back was almost too much for his youthful shoulders.

"Quite a load for a little boy!" the pastor smiled. Looking up into the kindly face of the older man, the red-cheeked boy exclaimed between the irregular puffs of breath: "Oh, he ain't heavy, Revrun, he's my brother!"

The pastor stood, as if transfixed, for a moment. And as the struggling boy faded into the gray of the gathering dusk, the pastor shook his head almost incredulously as he pondered: what a theme for a sermon!

"He ain't heavy, Revrun, he's my brother!"

What a different world this world would be if all of us took seriously the deeper implication of Christian brotherhood, if all of us were willing to look upon every human being as our physical brother, the creature of the same Creator, a fit subject for the full measure of our love.

And what a different church our church would be if all of us would look upon each fellow believer as a brother or sister in Christ. "Let brotherly love continue," the Scriptures admonish us (Heb. 13:1). "Love the brotherhood," St. Peter encourages (1 Peter 2:17). And to the members of this brotherhood the apostle Paul once wrote: "Bear ye one another's burdens, and so fulfill the Law of Christ." (Gal. 6:2)

It is the man whose heart has been warmed and strengthened by a daily consciousness of Christian brotherhood that can carry his needy fellow man upon his shoulders and look up into the face of God and say: "He's not heavy, Father, he's my *brother!*"

For the eternal miracle which made possible such unselfish love we must, of course, go back again and again to the manger in Bethlehem and to the cross on Calvary.

"Herein is love," the Bible tells us, "not that we loved God but that He loved us and sent His Son to be the Propitiation for our sins. Beloved, if God so loved us, we ought also to love one another." (1 John 4:10, 11)

Thank God for a Wastebasket!

$\mathbf{A}$ wise use of the waste-basket," says a distinguished editor, "is the secret of all successful editing." Perhaps only those who have spent years doing the work of an editor know how true that observation really is.

But a wise use of the wastebasket is the secret not only of successful editing; it is, in a sense, the secret of successful *living* too.

Too many lives are encumbered with rubbish that should have been discarded and thrown into the waste-basket long ago. Old worries, silly grudges, and smoldering resentments which should have been consigned to oblivion long since, are frequently held on to and nursed along from day to day as though we were afraid of losing or mislaying them.

There is only one place for the petty piques, the fester-ing feuds, and the smoldering grudges of yesterday. That place is in the wastebasket! We dare not permit the unholy emotions of yesterday to befoul the air of a fresh today or a new tomorrow.

What a difference there would be in the life of many a family, many a congregation, many an office, and many a factory if each of us had learned to purge himself of each unworthy thought and base emotion with every setting sun!

"Let not the sun go down upon your wrath," the Bible tells us, "neither give place to the devil" (Eph. 4:26, 27). Rather than give place to the devil, we are to put the devil in *his* place!

In another passage of Scripture we are told: "Let us *lay aside* every weight and the sin which doth so easily beset us" (Heb. 12:1). We are not to carry our besetting sins — our pet temptations, our pet prejudices, our pet grievances, and our pet worries — from one day into another. With God's help we are to *dispose* of them.

Happy indeed is the person who has learned to "lay aside," to "forget," the angry thoughts and base desires which pile up within his heart from day to day and to start each new morning unencumbered by a growing backlog of "wrongs to be righted" and "scores to be settled."

The apostle Paul had learned the blessed use of a wastebasket in the nurture of his own spiritual life. *"Forgetting* those things which are behind . . . I press toward the mark" (Phil. 3:13, 14), he tells us.

What an excellent thought at the dawning of each new day! Let us forget those things which God would have us forget, and let us press forward to those things which He would have us achieve.

Gone with the Wind

The story is told of a woman who once came to her pastor and confessed to him that she had become guilty of the sin of uncharitable gossip. Wasn't there something she could do to make amends for the wrong she had done? she asked.

After a moment's thought the pastor asked the troubled woman to accompany him up into the tower of the church. There he ripped open a pillow filled with goose feathers — and exposed the opened pillow to the winds.

Within a few minutes the pillow was empty, and the downy feathers were drifting all over the neighborhood, some here, some there, but many of them already beyond the sight of the woman in the church tower.

Turning to the perplexed woman, the pastor then instructed her to go out into the neighborhood, to regather the goose feathers, and to put them back into the pillow.

The assignment was impossible, of course, but no more impossible than it was for the troubled woman to recall the thoughtless words of idle gossip which she had spoken. Like the goose feathers, they had spread throughout the town and had gone beyond recall.

It lies in the very nature of slanderous gossip that, as a rule, there is no possible way of making satisfactory amends. If a man has stolen a dollar, he can pay it back in full. But if he has started a vicious rumor, he may repent and he may do his best to stop its spread, but usually he finds that the rumor has taken wings and has lodged in a thousand places, most of them beyond his reach.

There may be no way of making perfect restitution for the harm of thoughtless gossip but, thank God, there *is* a way of freeing the soul of gossip's guilt. He who "opened not His mouth" when He died for the sins of all mankind has won for us a glorious pardon also for those sins where, in our human frailty, we opened our mouth when we should have kept it closed.

Surely every one of us has reason to pray:

> Oh, let me never speak,
> What bounds of truth exceedeth;
> Grant that no idle word
> From out my mouth proceedeth;
> And then, when in my place
> I must and ought to speak,
> My words grant pow'r and grace
> Lest I offend the weak.

"The Heavens Declare . . ."

It was night. We were flying at an altitude of 19,000 feet. Below us was a floor of clouds, the under side of which was the ceiling of the town below. Above us was the diamond-studded canopy of heaven, twinkling with a myriad of stars.

Our traveling companion was a learned man. For quite some time he had impressed us with the various scientific reasons why everything we saw from our plane window could be explained *without a God.*

When the time came for us to reply, we were frankly at a loss. It was evident that we could match neither his scientific knowledge nor his technical vocabulary. And so we decided to reply as follows:

In our basement at home we have an automatic washer, at which we have never ceased to marvel. At just the right time this machine feeds just the right amount of water — just enough hot and just enough cold. At just the right time it transfers the suds to an adjoining tub, preserving them for a second use. At just the right time it sprinkles the clothes with clean, warm water for rinsing. At just the right time it spins them dry. And at just the right time it shuts the motor off.

Now, which assumption would be more reasonable? — to assume that a lot of bolts and nuts and washers swirled around in space until they decided to get together and become an automatic washer, precisely timed and purposefully planned? Or to assume that behind the washer there was a *mind,* a mind which conceived the delicate interrelation of all the various parts and which brought these parts together so that they would do exactly what the original mind intended?

As the discussion wore on, it seemed that our companion continued to be unimpressed. But long after the conversation had been concluded and we had drifted to another subject, he interrupted for a moment to observe: "By the way, *I've been thinking* about that wash machine of yours."

And as our graceful *Constellation* sped on through the night — with no light but that of the shimmering stars — we leaned back, looked out of our window, and mused: "The heavens declare the glory of God; and the firmament showeth His handiwork." (Ps. 19:1)

The Bug on the Windshield

It was a beautiful summer evening, still early enough for us to skim along a scenic highway in Southern Illinois without turning on the lights of our car.

We were in a hurry, and so we decided that we could wait until we got home to have the splatter removed from our windshield. As frequently happens on a summer evening, a large bug had collided with the glass in front of us, leaving an inelegant blotch to mark the spot of fatal contact.

But as we drove along, it seemed we just couldn't keep our eyes off that ugly spot. Indeed, again and again we found ourselves focusing our eyes to the short-range vision which ended on the pane of glass immediately before us. And each time we fixed our eyes on the ugly spot which was only a matter of inches away, we missed the beautiful panorama which lay at a distance before us.

The shades of night were falling, and as we crossed the crest of a familiar hill from which on other nights we had seen the shimmer of the evening star, we saw, instead, the splatter of a bug. It was so close, and in our perspective it was so large, that for a moment — for us, at least — there was no star.

How much this is like life, we thought. A bug bigger than the evening star! A bug big enough to blot out the rolling landscape of velvety green which stretched out for miles in front of us! It was all a matter of perspective, of course — a matter of fixing our eyes on the ugly thing that was closest to us, while we missed the vision of the beautiful and the abiding which surrounded us on every hand.

If only we could keep our eyes *off the bugs* on our windshields — the doubts and worries which beset our path from day to day, the petty piques, the irritations and vexations, the endless little preoccupations which loom so large in our lives and threaten to blot out the eternal stars of hope and love and faith!

And if only we could keep our eyes *on Him* who is "the Way" and on the immovable assurances which He has given us in His eternal Gospel! "I will lift up mine eyes unto the hills, from whence cometh my help; my help cometh from the Lord," says the psalmist. (Ps. 121:1,2)

That is the perspective, along which lies the spiritual landscape of joy and peace and faith and hope. Let us keep our eyes fixed on the hills of God's assurance. Let us keep them away from the bugs on our windshields.

"Our God Is at Both Ends"

The story is told of a farmer boy who was hauling his first load of hay to town. Perched midway up the mountain of hay which rose high above the wagon — and which bulged far on either side — he guided his horses along a few miles of country road until he came to a covered bridge.

The bridge was long. And, being walled in on both sides and covered with a wooden roof, it had the appearance of a darkened tunnel.

Pulling his horses to a stop at the very entrance to the bridge, the boy peered along its inside walls which seemed to close in funnellike as they converged on the small patch of light at the other end. Then he took an appraising look at the broad load he was carrying.

After a moment's deliberation, he shook his head and said: "Nope, I'll never make it. The other end's too narrow." And so he backed up, turned his horses around, and headed toward home.

The boy, of course, was the victim of an optical illusion. Had he gone on, he would have found that the enclosed bridge was just as broad at the far end as it was at the end where he was standing.

Life is *filled* with optical illusions! At the entrance to many a new day, as we looked along the inside walls of the hours before us, we wondered how we would ever be able to carry our burden past the evening-end of the bridge.

But when evening came, we found that the same Lord who was with us at the entrance to the day was still with us at its close. Again and again, as we laid the burdens of the finished day aside, we experienced the spiritual fulfillment of the prophet's words: "At evening time it shall be light." (Zech. 14:7)

And how often in the middle of the night, as we looked down the dark corridor of the hours before us, has our weak faith almost prayed that the sun would never dawn — lest once more its morning light bring our problems into bold relief!

And yet when morning came, we experienced the truth of the psalmist's words: "When I awake, I am still with Thee" (Ps. 139:18), or our heart was lifted by the strong assurance: "His mercies are new every morning." (Lam. 3:23)

No matter which end of the bridge we are standing on, we can be sure: our God is at *both* ends! And through Christ we have learned that He is not only the God of power and might and wisdom but also the God of love and grace and mercy.

On whatever end of the bridge we may be standing at this moment, let us put our hand in His — and go courageously forward.

Crooked Rivers

A little boy who was paging through his first geography asked his mother: "Why are all the rivers crooked?"

The answer, of course, is simple. Rivers are crooked because they follow the lines of least resistance.

The same rule is true of men. Our lives, as a rule, do not become crooked, warped, and out of joint, because we deliberately set out to make them that way, but rather because we do not have the moral courage to overcome the hundred and one temptations that cross our daily paths.

It's so much easier to *listen* to gossip than to *stop* it. So much easier to tell a lie than to tell the truth — and take the consequences.

It's so much easier to stay in bed an hour longer on Sunday morning than to get up and go to church. So much easier to settle down in an easy chair with the evening paper than to go to a meeting of the Sunday school teachers, the church council, or the mission committee.

Like the river which meanders *around* the boulders and skirts the granite ledges in order to make its lazy way through the unresisting sand, we find it so much easier to do the things which call for the least amount of moral effort.

Is it any wonder that so many lives are *crooked?* Is it any wonder that when God looks down from heaven upon the lives of men and compares them with the perfect rule of His divine commandments, He must say: "They are all gone *aside* . . . there is none that doeth good, no, not one"? (Ps. 14:3)

Like the rivers in the little boy's geography, many a life is terribly crooked — turning now to the left and then to the right, when God commands that we go forward.

There is only one Hope for a crooked life, and that is a perfect Savior. In Him all crookedness has been forgiven. In Him all crookedness can be made straight and all roughness can be made plain. (Is. 40:4)

Would you like to be through with crookedness? Through with these endless meanderings *around* the path of duty? Look to Christ at the dawn of each new day — and heed His kindly "Follow Me!"

The Canceled Debt

It is said that at one time in his life Henry Clay owed $10,000 to a bank in Kentucky. A number of sympathetic friends, knowing that Mr. Clay was troubled over his inability to pay, secretly raised the money and quietly paid off the debt.

When Mr. Clay later came to the bank to discuss his large indebtedness, the cashier startled him with the unexpected announcement: "Mr. Clay, your account has been paid in full!"

"Why, how am I to understand you?" Mr. Clay exclaimed.

"Well," said the cashier, "a number of your friends have raised a sufficient sum and have paid off your debt for you. You don't owe this bank a dollar."

Tears rushed into Mr. Clay's eyes and, unable to speak, he walked away. His heart was overwhelmed by the joy of a great deliverance — deliverance from a crushing debt.

What a striking illustration of the central fact of our most holy faith! It was just such a deliverance that St. Paul had in mind when he wrote to the Christians of his day:

"And you, being dead in your sins . . . hath He quickened . . . having forgiven you all trespasses; blotting out the handwriting of ordinances that was against us, which was contrary to us, and took it out of the way, nailing it to His cross." (Col. 2:13, 14)

The handwriting to which the apostle here refers was the immeasurable debt of unforgiven sin which stood against us in the court of heaven.

But that handwriting is now gone, the Bible tells us. It is destroyed, put aside, blotted out! Christ has *paid* the debt. "God was in Christ," the apostle tells us, "reconciling the world unto Himself, not imputing their trespasses unto them" (2 Cor. 5:19) — that is, not charging their sins to their account.

At the foot of the cross on Calvary lies the handwriting that once stood against us — blotted out, its accusations forever covered by the atoning blood of Jesus. And from heaven comes the divine acknowledgment, the receipt which God Himself has sealed forever by the resurrection of His Son: *"Paid in full! Forgiven through the Savior's blood!"*

It was this surpassing knowledge that inspired Horatius Bonar to write those words of humble yet exultant gratitude:

> Thy death, not mine, O Christ,
> Has paid the ransom due;
> Ten thousand deaths like mine
> Would have been all too few!

Are we spending every day of our lives in humble and grateful awareness of God's unmerited forgiveness — of His unbounded love that cancels all our sins?

"Please Do Not Disturb"

We were walking down the eighth-floor corridor of a Hollywood hotel. It was Sunday morning — a little after nine. On door after door we saw the familiar little placard: "Please do not disturb."

We couldn't help thinking of how accurately that little placard expressed the attitude of millions of Americans toward the claims of Christ and His Gospel.

Not only on Sunday mornings but every hour of the week the Son of God stands before human hearts with His age-old invitation and His gracious promise:

"Behold, I stand at the door and knock. If any man hear My voice and open the door, I will come in to him and will sup with him, and he with Me." (Rev. 3:20)

And every hour of the week there are people responding to this approach of the Savior by pointing to the little placard on the door of their heart — "Please do not disturb."

They have become so preoccupied with a thousand and one other things in life that they have chosen, consciously or unconsciously, not to be bothered.

But Christ just can't be brushed off that easily. If any man ever learned that to his complete dismay, it was the Roman Governor Pontius Pilate. Nothing would have suited him better on that first Good Friday morning than to hang out the neat little placard "Please do not disturb."

But Christ was there! Christ had to be dealt with! A decision had to be made, and it had to be made either "for" or "against."

We may sympathize with a man like Pilate who, when he found himself on the horns of a dilemma, asked again and again: "What shall I do, then, with Jesus?" But in the final analysis that is the question which confronts every man who ever comes face to face with the claims of Christ.

The Christ of Christmas, the Christ of Good Friday, and the resurrected Christ of Easter morning is inescapable. No modern man or woman can hope to remain "undisturbed" by this Crisis-character who was born and lived and died and rose again some two thousand years ago.

The most happy people in the world today are those who have been "disturbed" by the Bible's message of sin and judgment, who have been awakened from their spiritual sleep, and who live in daily awareness of the love of God in Christ Jesus, our Lord. On the doors of their hearts is inscribed the loving invitation:

> Redeemer, come! I open wide
> My heart to Thee; here, Lord, abide!
> Let me Thine inner presence feel,
> Thy grace and love in me reveal!

Pursuing the Trivial

There once was a dog named Sport, who started to chase a bear. Just as he came within a few yards of the bear, a fox suddenly crossed his path.

This turned his attention away from the bear, and immediately he set out in chase of the fox. When he was getting close to the fox, a rabbit ran out from a clump of bushes near him, and he began to chase the rabbit.

By this time Sport was panting hard. But just as he was about to catch the rabbit, a mouse ran into his path. And so he forgot about the rabbit and began to chase the mouse. He chased it up and down the field for nearly half a mile — when suddenly it disappeared into a hole.

Completely exhausted, poor Sport stood at the opening of the hole and barked — until he collapsed from exhaustion.

The story is only a parable, of course. But what a parable of the busy church of today! How often, at the end of a project which started out to achieve great things for Christ have we, as it were, found ourselves, exhausted, panting down a rat hole!

Somehow the big things that we set out to achieve — the high and holy purposes of Christ's kingdom — are successively replaced by smaller things, until finally our energies are completely dissipated in the mad pursuit of trivialities.

How many a venture of faith which was born in the prayerful atmosphere of the *upper* room has languished and died in the ash trays of the *supper* room! How many an organization which, at its inception, was dedicated to the spiritual improvement of its membership has ended up in a stack of dirty silverware and a sinkful of steaming dishwater!

Somewhere along the line someone got off the track. Like poor Sport who started out to catch a bear and then switched his attention to a fox and then a rabbit and then a mouse and finally died barking down a rat hole, they have permitted their big objective to be replaced by smaller ones until they have become completely absorbed in secondary aims.

Congregations, church societies, and individual Christians surely have every reason to emulate the singleness and tenacity of purpose which motivated the apostle Paul. "This *one thing* I do," he said. "Forgetting those things which are behind, and reaching forth unto those things which are before, I press toward the mark for the prize of the high calling of God in Christ Jesus." (Phil. 3:13, 14)

He who keeps his eyes on the highest goals is not likely to end up — *pursuing the trivial.*

"He Shall Be Like a Tree . . ."

Have you ever walked down a city street which was lined with stately sycamores? Rising high on either side, like pillars in a huge cathedral, they extend their leafy arms across the street — until they form a canopy of green, affording shade throughout the summer months.

At regular intervals among the sycamores there is a shabby telephone pole — splintered, gashed, and weather-beaten. Although it stands as erect as the sycamores, it sprouts no branches, shoots forth no leaves, and contributes nothing to the gorgeous symphony of green and brown and yellow which thrills the heart of every passer-by.

Why the difference? The answer, of course, is simple. The sycamores have roots, and the telephone poles have none. The sycamores have tapped an unseen source below the ground from which they draw their daily nourishment, while the telephone pole is merely a piece of lifeless wood sunk into the ground.

In a sense more real than may at first be apparent, the man who has put his faith in Christ is just like one of those sycamores. He has sunk his roots deep into the promises of God, and in those promises he has found the power which has transformed his life into a fresh and growing vital thing.

In the familiar words of the First Psalm, he is "like a tree planted by the rivers of water, that bringeth forth his fruit in his season; his leaf also shall not wither, and whatsoever he doeth shall prosper." (Ps. 1:3)

The Savior was doing more than painting a pretty word picture when He said: "I am the Vine. Ye are the branches. He that abideth in Me, and I in him, the same bringeth forth much fruit." (John 15:5)

He whose life has been firmly rooted in Christ, whose inmost thoughts go back again and again to the immovable assurances of the Savior's Gospel, is in daily contact with a source of power beyond the ability of mortal man to fathom.

That is why "his leaf also shall not wither." Like the graceful sycamore whose leaves are not only a thing of beauty but also a covering of shade for the hot and weary traveler, his life will be adorned by the foliage of Christian virtue and will bring comfort and joy into the hearts of others.

"Who Taught You to Swear?"

An elderly pastor was riding in the back seat of a horse-drawn coach. The driver, a fine-looking young man, had the wicked habit of swearing at his horses. For some time the clergyman was silent.

At length, however, he leaned forward and asked with a kindly voice: "Will you tell me, my friend, who taught you to swear? Was it your mother?"

The young man turned toward the pastor with a look of surprise. It was evident the older man had touched a tender spot. "My mother?" replied the driver. "Why, no, sir! My mother is a praying woman. It would break her heart if she ever heard me swearing."

Very pointedly, the old man then suggested that he honor not only the teachings of his Christian mother but also the commandment of his mother's God: "Thou shalt not take the name of the Lord, thy God, in vain."

"I thank you, Sir," the young man replied. And during the remainder of the journey not another oath was heard.

What the world (and many a Christian!) needs to be told again and again today is that profanity is not only a flouting of the wish of Christian mothers but also a transgression of the Law of God.

Cursing and swearing are sinful! There may be those

who feel they have not achieved full social poise until they have learned to curse and swear in public without blushing, but the fact remains: the profane man betrays not only his limited vocabulary, his emotional immaturity, and his general bad taste, but also his lack of respect for the Word and will of God. And that is sin.

St. James was speaking of the tremendous power of the tongue for good or evil when he wrote: "Therewith bless we God . . . and therewith curse we men. . . . Out of the same month proceedeth blessing and cursing. My brethren, these things ought not so to be." (James 3:9, 10)

Indeed, they *ought* not so to be! He who has been "redeemed to God" (Rev. 5:9) by the death of Jesus Christ, His Son, will never want to use the name of God in a disrespectful or unbecoming manner.

A Lantern in the Dark

It was a cold winter's night. Five-year-old Bobby held his father's hand tightly as they walked along a dark footpath which led to a neighboring farmhouse.

It was evident that Bobby was afraid — afraid of the pitch-black darkness which stretched out endlessly before him. Finally, looking at the lantern in his father's hand, he whimpered: "Daddy, I'm scared! The light reaches only such *a little way!*"

The father tightened his grip on the little boy's hand and answered with confident assurance: "I know, son. But if we just keep on walking, we'll see that the light keeps on shining all the way to the end of the road."

What a fitting parable for the Christian pilgrim as he leaves another day behind him and places his feet on the unknown road which lies ahead! To our heavenly Father you and I are little Bobbies — sometimes confident, but sometimes frightened by the inky darkness of the road before us. How often, in the blackness of our night, have we whimpered that the light which God has given us "reaches only such a little way!"

And how often have we found that if we just kept on walking in the light which He has given us, His light would keep on shining, illuminating each new step as we would take it. God has not given His believers a battery of klieg lights which light up each detail of the road which lies ahead, but He *has* given them a lantern in the darkness which, if they take heed to it, will illumine their entire pathway — step by step.

"Thy Word is a lamp unto my feet and a light unto my path" (Ps. 119:105). There is no darkness which cannot be pierced by that lamp. And in the light of that lamp we can take each new step with confidence.

There may be vast stretches of the road ahead which we cannot see, but the lamp of God's Word assures us that those stretches, just as the step which lies before us, will be illumined by His love.

"If we walk in the light," says St. John, "as He is in the light, we have fellowship one with another, and the blood of Jesus Christ, His Son, cleanseth us from all sin" (1 John 1:7). The light of God's lamp is the light of His love. His love, revealed to us in Bethlehem, on Calvary, and again in Joseph's garden, is the guarantee of our security.

"He that spared not His own Son, but delivered Him up for us all, how shall He not with Him also freely give us *all* things?" (Rom. 8:32). Surely, if we'll just keep walking in *His* light, He'll be with us — all the way.

"I Am Still with Thee . . ."

After a protracted illness a Christian woman was taken to the hospital for surgery. Noticing her distress as she was being prepared for the operation, an attendant took her hand and whispered softly:

"Madam, you have nothing to fear. Only one of two things could possibly happen to you — and both of them are good. If you should die, you will be with Jesus. If you should live, Jesus will be with you. In either case, both of you will be together."

What a precious comfort! In health or in sickness, in joy or in sorrow, in life or in death, both of them — Jesus and she — would always be together.

King David, whose life was a constant succession of tragedy and triumph, found strength and assurance in that thought. In Psalm 139 he exclaims: "How precious also are Thy thoughts unto me, O God! . . . *When I awake, I am still with Thee.*" (Ps. 139:17, 18)

That is the Christian's comfort in every dark moment. That is his comfort especially in the dark moments of illness. The night may be long and trying, the sleep fitful and feverish, the body faint, and the heart anxious; but no matter what the trials of the night may be — "when I awake, I am still with Thee." And to be with *Christ* — what greater comfort could there be?

[84]

And even after the night of life's little day is over, when the curtains of eternity are lifted and the Sun of Righteousness beams forth in all its healing brilliance — even then, in *death,* "when I awake, I am still with Thee!"

But we need not be sick or in trouble or in danger to experience the thrill and the joy of this constant and unbroken companionship. Every night of our lives, when the toils of the day are done and the lights are turned out and we lay our head upon our pillow to invite sweet rest and slumber — we can close our eyes in the confident asurance that "when I awake, I am still with Thee — either here in *my* home or else up there in *Thine.*"

There is nothing in life that can harm us if through faith in Christ the Savior we have placed ourselves, for time and for eternity, securely into the Father's hands. His presence will go with us in every circumstance of life — and in His presence no evil dare come nigh us.

Who Puts the Numbers Up?

It happened in a coffee shop in a Chicago hotel. A clergyman was finishing his breakfast when a man slid onto the stool beside him and nervously ordered "some rolls and a cup of coffee."

"Did you see that headline?" the stranger asked, as he pointed to a bold streamer across the morning paper: "Air Crash Kills 52."

"I'm supposed to catch a plane for Los Angeles this noon, and frankly I'm scared stiff. If I didn't have to be there for a meeting in the morning, I'd cancel my reservation and take the 'Chief.'"

As they sipped their coffee, they exchanged a few words on the relative safety of travel by air and by train. It so happened that the clergyman, too, had a plane reservation that very afternoon. He had a ticket for Buffalo, *and he intended to use it!*

"Well, I guess it's all in the way you look at it," mused the stranger. "When your number's up — it's up."

The minister looked at the frightened man a moment and then replied: "Yes — I suppose so. But I happen to know the Man who puts the numbers up."

The stranger put his cup down as though he were afraid he might drop it. Could his friend be joking? Or was he really serious? But before he could bring himself to ask, the minister continued:

"You see, the Man who puts the numbers up happens to be my Father."

And from there he went on to tell the stranger of the loving care and protection of his heavenly Father who has promised to keep him in all his ways. Both he and his "number" are in the Father's hand — and his number will not be "up" until his Father puts it there.

David, the psalmist, said something very much the same. "My times are in Thy hand" (Ps. 31:15), he said. As he looked back upon a life which had been lived very dangerously, he saw the protecting hand of God in every circumstance. And as he looked forward, he knew that the omnipotent hand of his heavenly Father would guide and guard him until his dying day.

It was he who ended his Twenty-third Psalm with the confident words: "Goodness and mercy shall follow me all the days of my life, and I will dwell in the house of the Lord forever." (Ps. 23:6)

Should we not have the same assurance? Our lives are in the hands of Him who lived and died that we might live. Those hands will never waver. And when someday our "number will be up" — thank God! *He will hold the number!*

A Study in Pronouns

It was a Christian school. The subject of the grammar lesson was pronouns. The teacher had told the children that "a pronoun is a word used instead of a noun."

As an illustration, she asked little Mary to read the fifty-third chapter of the prophet Isaiah, and to emphasize the pronouns as she read them.

This is what Mary read:

"Surely *HE* hath borne *OUR* griefs and carried *OUR* sorrows . . . *HE* was wounded for *OUR* transgressions; *HE* was bruised for *OUR* iniquities; the chastisement of *OUR* peace was upon *HIM,* and with *HIS* stripes *WE* are healed. . . . The Lord hath laid on *HIM* the iniquity of *US* all." (Is. 53:4-6)

Perhaps little Mary didn't realize it at the time, but in those simple words she had preached the sublimest and the profoundest sermon ever preached. The Christian message is, in a sense, a message of pronouns.

He — for us!

"Christ died for us," the Scriptures tell us (Rom. 5:8). "God made Him to be sin for us who knew no sin" (2 Cor. 5:21). "He died for all, that they which live should not henceforth live unto themselves, but unto Him which died for them, and rose again" (2 Cor. 5:15). What blessed pronouns!

Christ — instead of me!

"God commendeth His love toward us in that, while we were yet sinners, Christ died for us" (Rom. 5:8). "He His own self bare our sins in His own body on the tree" (1 Peter 2:24). "He loved me — and gave Himself for me!" (Gal. 2:20)

The Christian Gospel is, above all else, a message of substitution. Christ, the eternal Son of the living God, took our place; He suffered our punishment; He died in our stead; He paid our debt; He secured for us a place in the everlasting mansions of His Father.

> Upon a life I did not live,
> Upon a death I did not die;
> Another's life, Another's death,
> I stake my whole eternity!

His — "Twice-Over"

The story is told of a little boy who spent many days making himself a sailboat.

When the boat was finished, he took it down to the stream to see if it would sail. Proudly he walked along the river bank as his little craft glided, erect, on the rippled waters — its white sail curved to the summer breeze.

But to his consternation the ship soon headed out to the middle of the stream — too far for him to reach — and gradually disappeared from sight. It was a heart-broken lad who returned to his home that evening.

Weeks later he saw his sailboat in a pawnshop window — the very boat which he had made and rigged and painted with such meticulous care! He asked the operator of the pawnshop if he could have the boat, but his heart sank when the man replied: "Only if you pay the price which is marked on this little tag."

For weeks the lad worked to earn the price of the boat. Finally, with the money in his hand, he returned to the pawnshop, placed the money on the counter, and said: "Please, Mister, I'd like to have my boat."

And as he left the store with the boat in his hands, he looked at it with that feeling of pride and joy and affection which little boys lavish on the creations of their own fingers, and said: "You're mine, little boat! You're mine twice-over! Once, because I *made* you. Twice, because I *bought* you!"

The analogy may be imperfect, as most analogies are — but the way that little boy felt about his boat is the way God feels about you and me.

The Bible tells us: "It is He that hath *made* us" (Ps. 100:3). It tells us furthermore: "Ye are *bought* with a price (1 Cor. 6:20). And it even tells us about the price which was paid to buy us back: "Ye are redeemed (bought back) with the precious blood of Christ." (1 Peter 1:19)

What a comfort it is to know that beyond the reaches of this universe there is a Father in heaven who looks down upon you and me and says: "You are Mine, little man — little woman. You are Mine twice-over. Once, because I *made* you. Twice, because I *bought* you."

A Sermon from a Train Window

We were traveling from Los Angeles to St. Louis. The floodwaters in the Midwest had reached a new high. Farmlands and highways lay beneath a murky lake which stretched as far as our eyes could see.

Slowly and cautiously the crack streamliner made its way into what seemed to be a trackless and bottomless lake. Would it sink into the deep? Would it lose its way? Was it headed for disaster?

Confidently the engineer headed the nose of the graceful Diesel into the swirling waters. He knew that only a few inches below the surface of the flood were solid tracks — invisible to the eye.

Because he had gone that way a hundred times before, he knew that the unseen tracks were well able to hold his train above the water — and that they would lead him to dry land just a mile or two ahead.

And so, as we looked from our train window, we were startled by the illusion of a heavy streamliner sailing gracefully across the surface of the surging floodtide!

What a picture of the Christian life, we thought! And we were reminded of the word of Scripture: "The eternal God is thy Refuge, and *underneath are the everlasting arms*" (Deut. 33:27). Underneath were the solid roadbed, the sturdy ties, the heavy spikes, and the unbending rails of steel.

He who has found forgiveness for his sins through faith in Jesus Christ, his Savior, can launch out upon a trackless future, confident that "underneath are the everlasting arms."

He knows that through Christ the almighty God has become his strong Protector. The floodwaters of adversity, the storms of trial, the winds and waves of sore distress may threaten to throw him off his course — but he is riding on solid tracks, tracks which have been forged and fashioned by God Himself and which lead through the gathering waters to the safe, dry land ahead.

The everlasting arms which are always underneath can be seen only by the eyes of faith. But he who has once seen them — can walk upon the floods!

Revealed by His Footprint

A Frenchman was crossing the desert with an Arab guide. Day after day the Arab knelt on the burning sand and called upon his God.

At last, one evening when the Arab knelt to pray, the unbelieving Frenchman asked the Arab: "How do you know there *is* a God?"

The guide fixed his eyes upon the scoffer for a moment and then replied: "How do I know there is a God? I'll answer that question, if you permit me to ask you one first. How did we know this morning that it was a camel and not a man that had passed our tent while we slept last night?"

The Frenchman laughed his reply: "Why, we could tell it by the print of the hoof in the sand. That print was not from the foot of a man."

The Arab then looked to the West where the setting sun threw shafts of red and gold and purple into the vaulted canopy of heaven, and pointing toward the sun, he said: "Neither is *that* the footprint of a man."

The world about us is *filled* with the footprints of God! Every sunset, every sunrise, every twinkling star in the diamond-studded ceiling which envelopes this marvelous world of ours — is a footprint of our Maker.

The Bible tells us: "The heavens declare the glory of God; and the firmament showeth His handiwork" (Ps.

19:1). He who can see the scarlet sun sink into its pool of purple, splashing the sky with streaks of gold and crimson — and still not see the footprint of his Maker — is like a pair of spectacles without a pair of eyes behind them.

But God has not left us to follow the path to Him by footprints. He has *revealed* Himself to us through the pages of His Word. The book of nature may tell us that there is a God, but only the Book of Books can tell us who He is — and what He has done for us through Jesus Christ, His Son.

The footprints of the setting and the rising sun may tell us that God *is*. But only the nailprints in the hands of our Redeemer can tell us that God is — *Love*.

Not Better — But "Better Off"

A scoffing soldier was making fun of his buddy who was a sincere believer in Christ. "The trouble with you Christians," said the scoffer, "is that you think you are better than the rest of us."

"Not better," replied the Christian young man, "just better *off*."

How true! The man who has been brought into a right relationship with God through faith in Christ, the Savior, is *indeed* better off than the man who has not.

Any person who has become a "new man" in Christ and who in the power of his risen Lord leads a Christian life, is much better off than the person who turns his back on the Gospel offer and determines to "go it on his own."

"Godliness is profitable unto all things," the Bible tells us, "having promise of the life that *now is* and of that which is to come" (1 Tim. 4:8). The godly man need not wait until heaven to be better off — he is better off here and now!

His rewards may not be those of financial success and social standing. Perhaps no one at the local bank would ever rate him better off than hundreds of depositors whose monthly balances are ten times greater than his.

Nowhere has God told us that godliness holds promise of material success. But He *has* told us that, unfailingly, the rewards of humble trust in Christ and His Gospel are: peace, joy, assurance, the victorious inner life, and, finally, eternal life with Him in heaven.

To know every morning that we have a Savior who has promised to be with us "always, even unto the end of the world" (Matt. 28:20), and to know every evening, when we invite sweet sleep to erase the scars of another day, that we have a Savior who has died to restore us to sonship with His Father — such knowledge is indeed a blessing for which we have no measurement.

Our daily sins may convince us that we are no better than many of our fellow men; but God's daily grace will convince us, beyond all doubt, that we are better *off!*

It was this knowledge that prompted the poet to write:

> Perish every fond ambition,
> All I've sought or hoped or known;
> Yet how rich is my condition —
> God and heaven are still my own!

To Heaven on a Pass?

John had put the question somewhat irreverently, but the question had hit the mark, "Do you mean that I can get to heaven *on a pass?*"

Somewhat surprised at this unusual language, the pastor thought a while and then replied: "Yes, John. In fact, that is the *only* way you can get there. There are no 'paid admissions.' Whoever gets to heaven gets there on a pass."

"But it just isn't reasonable!"

"I know," smiled the elderly clergyman. "God didn't consult us in arranging His plan of salvation, and let's thank Him that He didn't. I'm sure none of us would have thought up a plan so wonderful as His.

"The apostle Paul couldn't figure out all the whys and wherefores which lay behind God's marvelous plan. That's why he exclaimed:

" 'Oh, the depth of the riches both of the wisdom and knowledge of God! . . . Who hath known the mind of the Lord? Or who hath been His counselor?' (Rom. 11:33-36)

"But let's come back to your somewhat unusual expression once more. St. Paul wrote an entire book of the Bible, the Letter to the Romans, to show that no man could possibly 'buy his ticket' to heaven. That is, no man could possibly get there by his own efforts, his own goodness or morality.

"In fact, he claimed that no man could even make a partial payment on his own ticket — or co-operate with God in any way in the purchase of his salvation. He said that entrance into heaven was only 'by pass' — only by grace — only by trusting the shed blood of Jesus Christ, God's Son.

"Here, let's read Romans 3:20 to 28. . . ."

We may not be ready to use John's language about getting to heaven on a pass, but his question showed that he had understood the Christian doctrine of justification by faith — the doctrine that a man gets to heaven, not because of any merit of his own, but solely and alone through faith in the substitutionary life and death and resurrection of the Savior.

> Just as I am, without one plea
> But that Thy blood was shed for me
> And that Thou bidd'st me come to Thee,
> O Lamb of God, I come.

The Practice of His Presence

The story is told of a pious Scotsman who was suffering from a critical illness. One day he was visited by the new minister who had only recently been called to his parish.

After the pastor had seated himself by the sick man's bedside, he noticed a vacant chair which had been pulled up on the other side of the bed and which had evidently been used just before he entered the room.

Pointing to the vacant chair, the pastor said: "Well, I see I'm not your *first* visitor this morning."

Following the pastor's eye to the vacant chair, the old man replied: "Oh — that chair? Let me tell you about it.

"Many years ago I found it impossible to pray when I went to bed. I often fell asleep on my knees; I was so tired. And if I managed to keep awake, I couldn't keep my thoughts from wandering.

"One day I spoke to the minister about it. He told me not to worry about kneeling down. 'Just *sit* on your bed,' he said, 'and put a chair opposite you. Imagine that Jesus is in it, and talk to Him just as you would to a friend.'

"I began doing that," the Scotsman continued. "And I've been doing it ever since. So now you know why the chair is standing there like that."

It wasn't many days later when the old man's daughter came running to the minister's home. "Father died last night," she said through her tear-moistened eyes. "I had no idea death was so near. He seemed to be sleeping so comfortably. And when I went back to see if everything was all right, he was dead.

"He hadn't moved since I saw him a few minutes before, except that — *his hand was out on the empty chair at the side of his bed."* ...

It may not be possible, or even desirable, for us to cultivate the habit of the vacant chair; but how important it is that every one of us, like the Scotsman, cultivate the practice of the Savior's presence. In life and in death we shall be blessed beyond measure if we have learned to place our hand in His.

Let us then each morning and again each night, by a conscious act of faith, put our hand in His. For then we shall be able to say with the psalmist: "Yea, though I walk through the valley of the shadow of death, I will fear no evil, for *Thou art with me!"* (Ps. 23:4)

What a Friend!

The teacher was leading her class in a study of definitions. She would read the respective words, and the children would give their own definitions — each in his turn.

It seemed all the children were well prepared on this particular morning. One after another gave his own definition of uncle, aunt, cousin, neighbor, much to the delight not only of the teacher but also of the whole class, which took pride in their group achievement.

When it came to little Jimmy's turn, however, it looked for a moment as though their splendid record would be broken. Jimmy was the first to hesitate and to fumble. The word which he was to define was the simple word "friend," and somehow, try as hard as he would, he could think of no way of defining this familiar word.

Finally, after desperate mental effort, he blurted out his childlike definition of a friend. "A friend," he said, "is someone who likes us, even though he knows us!"

Perhaps little Jimmy's definition will never be included in any dictionary, yet it contains insights which are not contained in many formal definitions of this simple word. For is it not a part of the essence of friendship that one person continues to "like" another despite his evident faults and shortcomings? Truly, a friend *is* a person who likes us, even though he knows us!

How true that is especially of the friendship which exists in the heart of God and which goes out to all His fallen creatures. He knows us for what we are, and *yet* He loves us. Indeed, no one knows us better and yet loves us more.

St. Paul tells us that "God commendeth His love toward us in that, while we were yet sinners, Christ died for us" (Rom. 5:8). In the very same chapter we are told that Christ died for those whom He knew to be ungodly.

If it is true, as little Jimmy said, that "a friend is someone who likes us, even though he knows us," then what a Friend we have in Jesus!

"Jesus knows our every weakness" — and yet His heart goes out to us in pity, compassion, and affection.

He who said: "Greater love hath no man than this, that a man lay down his life for his friends" (John 15:13), proved the immeasurableness of His love by going out and dying even for His enemies!

What a Friend!

Barging In on Christmas?

It was a cold November morning. Two women, their arms filled with bundles and their coat collars raised against the wintry wind, were walking past the window of a large downtown department store.

In the window was a life-size tableau of the scene of the Nativity: the Christ Child in the manger, Mary and Joseph, the kneeling shepherds, and the cattle standing nearby.

"Can you beat that!" one of the women was overheard to say. "The churches are even barging in on Christmas!"

To her the substitution of the Christ Child for Kris Kringle was an unwarranted intrusion by the religious people of the community. What irony — that the world should have drifted so far from the original significance of the Christmas season that the King of Kings should be accused of "barging in" on His own birthday party!

What the world needs today is more — and not less — of such "barging in" on the part of the church. During these weeks let Christian people remember that the message of the season is in great part a missionary proclamation: "Behold, I bring you good tidings of great joy, which shall be to *all people.*" (Luke 2:10)

"All people," including the millions of busy shoppers who are milling through the crowded aisles of our department stores during these days, need to be told that

[104]

unto them is born a Savior. They need nothing more than that the church "barge in" on their preoccupation with the toys and tinsel of the season.

And who will deny that many a Christian home would benefit if during the weeks before and after Christmas it would permit the church and its message of pardon and peace through the Christ Child to play a more important part in its family celebration?

Will ours be just another Xmas — celebrated with the triple "X" of extravagance, excitement, and exhaustion? Or will it be a truly Christian Christ-mas, celebrated in the company of Him whose birth these days commemorate?

It will be the latter in the measure in which we permit the Honored Guest of Christmas to occupy our hearts — at home, at church, at work, and at play.

> Redeemer, come, I open wide
> My heart to Thee; here, Lord, abide!

Mount Sin and Mount Grace

Have you ever driven along a highway next to a mountainside? As you looked up, you could see nothing but mountains. It seemed the steep ascent was endless. But an hour later, when you were thirty or forty miles away, you looked back and saw that mountain in its true perspective.

Towering high above it, still farther in the background, rose a majestic mountain peak which literally dwarfed the smaller mountain which had looked so large — when you were so close.

There is a spiritual counterpart to this in the life of every Christian. As we look back, at the turn of every year, over the path which we have traveled, there loom up before our eyes, as it were, two great mountain peaks: the mountain of our sin and the mountain of God's grace.

Mount Sin is always there! How we hate it! How we deplore it! The past year, we must confess it to our shame, has again been a year of sin — of many sins, of grievous sins — on the part of every one of us. Standing high on the horizon which stretches out behind us is the frightening heap of our accumulated transgressions.

But towering high above it, unexcelled in glory and in grandeur, is the thrilling sight of *Mount Grace*. Our sins during the past year may have been great indeed. God's grace has been even greater. The ugly stain of our sin may have spread far and wide, but the healing shadow of His overpowering grace has spread even farther.

Indeed, just as in the evening hour the smaller mountain melts away in the shadow of the greater, so to the eye of the trusting child of God Mount Sin is forever being swallowed up in the shadow of Mount Grace. In the shadow of God's grace *all* sin must disappear.

In a sense the apostle Paul was speaking of Mount Sin and Mount Grace, when he wrote to his Roman Christians: "Where sin abounded, grace did much more abound" (Rom. 5:20). Sin was great. But grace was greater!

Let us, then, cross the threshold of the new year with these two all-pervading thoughts in mind: deep repentance for our personal sin and humble trust in divine grace; absolute despair of our own record of accomplishment, but absolute and unwavering confidence in that Savior whose record of accomplishment has been written to *our* credit — and who will be our Savior in the new year even as He has been in the old.

This Side of Heaven

As we write these lines, we are seated at the window of a speeding Pullman car — crossing the plains of Wyoming. It is late and almost time to retire. A few moments ago we were sitting alone in the darkness of our roomette, looking out into the blackness which has fallen like a shroud upon the world.

The night is clear, and the sky is a shimmering vault of velvet — with myriads of tiny windows letting bits of light peek through, as it were, from a land that knows no night. We thought, as we looked out of our fast-moving window, of that little girl who, reflecting on the splendor of a summer sky, looked up into her father's face and said: "Daddy, if the *wrong* side of heaven is so beautiful, how wonderful the *right* side must be!"

No human tongue or pen has ever succeeded in describing the glory, the grandeur, and the magnificence of the Father's house above. That it is a place of entrancing beauty and matchless splendor the apostle John indicates in the Book of Revelation by interpreting heaven's glories in terms of costly jewels and precious gems and rarest metals.

How could heaven be anything else but beautiful! It is the habitation of our God, the royal palace of our King! And in that palace — O wondrous thought! — our Savior has gone to prepare a place for us. Through faith in Him we shall ascend someday to His beautiful home beyond the skies — more exquisite, more glorious, more wonderful than human speech can tell! . . .

The train is speeding on — on into the night. Somewhere up in front there is a man who will stay awake after we have gone to sleep and, if it be God's will, he will bring us safely to our destination.

In a moment we shall put our typewriter away and shall retire for the night. But before we close our eyes in sleep, we shall look out once more from our pillow — out into the inky night — up to the shining windows of heaven — and pray:

> Lord Jesus, who dost love me
> Oh, spread Thy wings above me,
> And shield me from alarm!
> Though evil would assail me,
> Thy mercy will not fail me.
> I rest in Thy protecting arm.

Standing on God's Promises

In the early days of our country a weary traveler came to the banks of the Mississippi River for the first time. There was no bridge. It was early winter, and the surface of the mighty stream was covered with ice. Could he *dare* cross over? Would the uncertain ice be able to bear his weight?

Night was falling, and it was urgent that he reach the other side. Finally, after much hesitation and with many fears, he began to creep cautiously across the surface of the ice on his hands and knees. For he thought that thus he might distribute his weight as much as possible and keep the ice from breaking beneath him.

About half way over he heard the sound of singing behind him. Out of the dusk there came a colored man, driving a horse-drawn load of coal across the ice and singing merrily as he went his way!

Here he was — on his hands and knees, trembling lest the ice be not strong enough to bear him up! And there, as if whisked away by the winter's wind, went the colored man, his horses, his sleigh, and his load of coal — upheld by the same ice on which *he* was creeping!

Like this weary traveler, some of us have learned only to *creep* upon the promises of God. Cautiously, timidly, tremblingly we venture forth upon His promises, as though the lightness of our step might make His promises more secure. As though we could contribute even in the slightest to the strength of His assurances!

He has promised to be with us. Let us believe that promise! He has promised to uphold us. Let us believe Him when He says so. He has promised to grant us victory over all our spiritual enemies. Let us trust His truthfulness. Above all, He has promised to grant us full and free forgiveness of all our sins because of Jesus Christ, our Savior. And He has promised to come and take us to His heavenly home. Let us take Him at His word.

We are not to *creep* upon these promises as though they were too fragile to uphold us. We are to *stand* upon them — confident that God is as good as His word and that He will do what He has pledged.

It was this thought that the apostle Paul had in mind when he wrote to his Corinthians: "Stand fast in the faith! Quit you like men! Be strong!" (1 Cor. 16:13). — Don't creep.

A Friend in the Father's House

Few memories of childhood are more vivid in later years than those melancholy moments when, having offended our father by some childish misdemeanor, we were "afraid to go home."

What would Father say? What would Father do? Would there be any escaping the dreaded punishment? If only someone at home, perhaps Mother, perhaps big Brother, would take our part. If only someone would put in a word for us and would incline our father to forgive and to forget!

If only there were someone in our father's house who understood!

There *is* such a Person in our Father's house above. At this very moment He is "taking our part." At this very moment He is "putting in a word for us" and is pleading with His Father (and ours) to forgive us.

This Friend in the Father's house, of course, is Jesus. "My little children," says John, "if any man sin, we have an Advocate [one who speaks for us] with the Father, Jesus Christ, the Righteous" (1 John 2:2). Of this great Friend of sinners we are told in Hebrews: "He is able to save them to the uttermost that come to God by Him, seeing He ever liveth to make intercession for them." (Heb. 7:25)

He who on Calvary's cross, while dying for the sins of all mankind, exclaimed: "Father, *forgive* them!"

(Luke 23:34) still looks down in love upon His believing children and still is pleading before His Father's throne on high: "Father, *forgive* them!"

All our worries, all our anxieties, all our fears that stem from a guilty conscience and that make us afraid to step into the holy presence of our heavenly Father, can be put to rest. Next to our Father's throne stands our Elder Brother, who has suffered and died that we might live, and who has risen again and ascended to His home on high, there to put in an *eternal word* for us!

> He lives to bless me with His love,
> He lives to plead for me above. . . .
> He lives to calm my troubled heart,
> He lives all blessings to impart!

"It Fits Them All!"

Little Linda's eyes were big as saucers as she leaned on the kitchen table and exclaimed: "Oh, Mamma! It fits them all!"

She had been kneeling on a chair, next to the table, watching her mother pour hot liquid jelly into an assortment of containers — jelly glasses, mason jars, tumblers, and even a stemmed goblet which had been in the family for years.

To Linda's active little mind it was nothing short of a miracle that the formless liquid which her mother was ladling from the large aluminum kettle could at once assume the exact form of each container — the small glass, the large jar, the wide tumbler, and the bulging goblet.

And so in her simplicity she exclaimed: "Oh, Mamma! It fits them all!"

So, too, does God's grace fit every day — in the life of the believer! Our days, as it were, are like Linda's mother's assortment of containers — no two of them alike. Some of our days are twisted grotesquely by disappointment and discouragement. Some are flat with the monotonous humdrum of colorless routine. Some are high with spiritual adventure and achievement. And some are deep with doubt and dark despair.

But God's grace is sufficient for all of them (2 Cor. 12:9). His grace floods every corner of our lives. His grace takes the shape of each new day, for He has promised that as our days, so shall our strength be.

There is not a single corner of our lives, no matter how small, how secret, or how secluded, into which His healing love won't flow — if we will only let it.

Indeed, it is part of the miracle of God's grace that, after it has flooded and filled each new day, there is always some "still left over." The apostle Paul tells us: "Where sin abounded, grace did much *more* abound." (Rom. 5:20)

Not only does the love of God fill our every day, according to its needs; but as each succeeding day is finished and ready to be put away, God's love is still there, ready to fill the next.

Let us therefore not be fearful of tomorrow; for when tomorrow's sun will dawn, God's grace will still be able to fill our every need. "It fits them all!"

"If I Would Love Him More . . ."

An eminent artist had spent weeks painting a life-size picture of the Savior. One day, as he was adding the last delicate touches to the Master's face, a woman entered his room, unnoticed, and, standing at a distance, watched him in silence.

When the artist became aware of her presence, she finally broke her silence and remarked reverently: "You surely must love Him!"

Stepping back from his work and looking at it almost wistfully, the painter replied: "Love Him? Indeed I do!" And after a moment's hesitation he added: "But if I would love Him more, I would paint Him better!"

"If I would love Him more, I would paint Him better!"

In a very real sense it is part of the Christian's calling that he "paint Christ" for his fellow men. St. Peter says: "Ye are a chosen generation, a royal priesthood, a holy nation, a purchased people: that ye should show forth the virtues of Him who hath called you out of darkness into His marvelous light." (1 Peter 2:9 RSV)

It is the very purpose of Christ's people that they show forth the virtues of their Redeemer in the midst of an unbelieving world. By word and deed they are to acquaint men with the wonders of His love and the redeeming power of His death upon the cross.

[116]

What kind of picture of the Savior are we painting for our friends and neighbors — those who see us day by day? Is it the picture *He* would have us paint? Or is it a caricature of the Lord of Glory?

Perhaps some of us will have to confess with the artist: "If I would love Him more, I would paint Him better." If I would love Him more deeply, live with Him more intimately, speak to Him more frequently, listen to Him more attentively, obey Him more implicitly — I would reflect the power of His love more radiantly and more gloriously.

Indeed, every one of us might well fix the eyes of our faith upon the Christ whom we adore, and pray:

> Beautiful Savior, King of Creation,
> Son of God and Son of Man!
> Truly I'd love Thee, Truly I'd serve Thee,
> Light of my soul, my Joy, my Crown.

Mission Sermon on the Mount

Last night we stood high on a mountain overlooking the sprawling city of Greater Los Angeles. Beneath us, spreading as far to the left and as far to the right as we could see, lay a sight which defies description.

Like necklaces of shimmering jewels, the lights of the city sparkled brightly against the velvety black of a summer's night. There was no sound, yet in the distance we could see thousands of tiny lights moving slowly in all directions, criss-crossing one another in a dazzling tapestry of light and darkness.

These tiny lights creeping in the distance, we knew, were cars — each going somewhere at this late hour, and each carrying its precious human cargo.

And in the vast patches of black which lay between the golden strands there were darkened homes, invisible and silent. In these homes were four million people, many of them asleep, for the hour was getting late.

As we stood there, we thought of those words of Scripture, recorded in the Gospel according to St. Luke: "And when He was come near, He beheld the city and wept over it" (Luke 19:41). There was something somber, something melancholy about that sight.

Of the millions whose frantic little lives were being lived on the glittering stage which stretched before our view, how many were living in the darkness of spiritual night? How many were sleeping the sleep of spiritual death? How many were prepared to meet their God?

We thought, too, of God's description of this darkened world and of the great command which He has given to the members of His church:

"Arise, shine!" He says, "for thy Light is come, and the glory of the Lord is risen upon thee. For, behold, the darkness shall cover the earth, and gross darkness the people; but the Lord shall arise upon thee, and His glory shall be seen upon thee." (Is. 60:1, 2)

Twenty-four hours have passed since we stood there on the mountain, but somehow the picture and the message continue with us. To us they shall always be our — *mission sermon on the mount.*

A Funeral Wreath in Heaven

At one time in his life Martin Luther was extremely depressed and found it difficult to conceal his melancholy mood.

Soon he noticed that his faithful wife, Kate, had put on her mourning garments and had adopted an unaccustomed attitude of somber silence.

When he asked the reason for this sudden change, she replied quite simply: "Why, I thought that God had died — the way that you've been acting; and so I thought it proper that I should 'go in mourning.'"

How often have *we* gone about our daily tasks as though there were a funeral wreath on our Father's house above — as though our heavenly Father had died and had left us to shift for ourselves as best we could!

How often have we plodded along our pilgrim path as though our Father's house were empty — as though there were no living, loving Father there to care for us, to guide us, and to shield us with His mercy!

In days of sorrow and adversity, in days of problems and perplexities, let us remember that through Christ we have become "the sons of God," — the *living* God. We are God's children. Not God's orphans!

The Scriptures tell us that "our God is in the heavens," and that with Him "nothing shall be impossible." He who gave us the choicest jewel of heaven, His only-begotten Son — shall He not also give us those few temporal gifts which we need to support and sustain our earthly life?

He who charts the courses for the sun, the moon, the stars — shall He not also find a way for us?

No, there is no funeral wreath in heaven! Our Father is still in the Father's house. And because He *is,* our Savior tells us:

"Seek not what ye shall eat or what ye shall drink, neither be ye of doubtful mind. . . . Your Father *knoweth* that ye have need of these things." (Luke 12:29, 30)

> Lord, give us such a faith as this;
> And then, whate'er may come,
> We'll taste e'en now the hallowed bliss
> Of an eternal home.

"Such a Little Way Together"

They were at the family supper table. Mary was telling of an exasperating experience she had had on the way home from work that evening.

"This woman got on the bus at 55th," she said, "and squeezed into a small space right beside me. There she sat — half on top of me, and her bundles always poking me in the face. I had to keep dodging most of the time so that the one bundle wouldn't knock my hat off."

At that point Mary's little brother piped up: "Why didn't you tell her that she was half on *your* seat — and that she should get up?"

"It wasn't worthwhile," replied Mary, "we had such a little way to go together."

Mary, of course, didn't realize it at the time, but in those words she had expressed a philosophical (yes, theological) thought which well might serve as a motto for all of us. "It wasn't worthwhile; we had such a little way to go together."

How relatively unimportant the vexations and irritations of the day become when, at eventide, we view them in their true perspective. The unkindness, the ingratitude, the lack of understanding on the part of our fellow men — how much easier it is to bear them silently when we remember that "we have such a little way to go together"!

And how much more urgent does it become that we, on the other hand, show patience, forbearance, and sweet reasonableness to those who are making life's journey hand in hand with us — whenever we remind ourselves that "we have such a little way to go together."

We have so little time to show forth the virtues of Him who has called us out of darkness into His marvelous light! So little time to demonstrate the love of Him who first loved us! So little time to *live* His Gospel!

What a different world this world would be, what a different church our church would be, what a different family most of our families would be, if each of us would always remember: we have such a little way to go together!

The Wrong Start

Mommie, my coat's wrong!"

Four-year-old Betty had been struggling valiantly with the buttons on her new winter coat. Finally, after great effort, she thought she was finished. She had successfully poked each button through a hole.

But to her surprise and dismay there was still a buttonhole "left over"! And in her childish reasoning she concluded that whoever had made the coat had made a mistake.

There had been a mistake all right. But the mistake was not the tailor's. It was little Betty's. She had poked her *first* button into the wrong hole — and, of course, every button after that was wrong.

Betty had to be taught the importance of that very first button. If she would put *that* one into its proper place, all the rest would be comparatively simple.

And Betty's mother learned something too. There were a lot of other things in life in which it was important that Betty avoid the wrong start. It is always possible to unbutton a coat and to start all over, but it is *not* always possible to unbutton a life and to make a new beginning.

The habits which Betty is forming today are establishing the pattern of her habits tomorrow. If these habits are wrong the time to correct them is now. It will be much more difficult later.

Christian parents know how important it is that their children "get that first button right." They realize the truth of the Scriptural command and promise: "Train up a child in the way he should go; and when he is old, he will not depart from it." (Prov. 22:6)

That is why they bring their children to Christ in early infancy and surround them with a wholesome Christian influence throughout their childhood. That is why, as early in life as possible, they seek to place their children's feet upon the paths of faith and righteousness.

With God's help they want to give their children *the right start.*

God's Evergreens

On a wooded hillside in southern Illinois stood a mammoth evergreen.

In the springtime, when other trees were dressing themselves in their Easter finery, this evergreen seemed somewhat out of place. In the noontime of summer it was so much like the trees around it that it seemed to be lost in the landscape. And when autumn decked its neighbors in gorgeous garments of gold and red and purple, it seemed to be the most drab and lifeless of all the trees on the hillside.

But when *winter* had come and the other trees, stripped of their foliage, were waving their skeleton arms in the wind, then the humble evergreen stood out in all its verdant beauty. Even with the snow bending its drooping boughs, it was just as green, just as graceful, as it had been in the full flush of summer.

We often thought, as we drove our 1929 Chevrolet along the winding highway which skirted the edge of the hillside, how strikingly that evergreen symbolized the spiritual vigor and vitality of the Christian life.

The believer in Christ is, in a sense more real than may at first be apparent, one of God's evergreens. "His leaf *also* shall not wither" (Ps. 1:3). In the winter seasons of life, when the winds blow stiff and strong, when the dull gray skies of gloom and sorrow shut out the rays of cheering sunshine, the Christian stands out among his fellows as one of God's evergreens.

The source of his strength is God's love. And God's love knows no spring or summer or autumn or winter. It is ever constant, ever availing. With God's love, as with God Himself, there is no change or variableness. For He has revealed His love to us through Jesus Christ, the Savior, who is the same yesterday, today, and forever.

Come sunshine or sorrow, good fortune or calamity, delight or distress — the Christian has found a source of spiritual nourishment unknown to his fellows. He has sunk his roots deep into the spoken promises of God. And from these assurances he draws daily strength to adorn his life with Christian virtues — no matter what the circumstance.

The believers in Christ are indeed God's evergreens.

The Best Translation

 Four clergymen were discussing the relative merits of the various translations of the Bible.

One liked the King James Version best because of its beautiful and classical English. Another liked the American Revised Version best because it is more literal and comes closer to the original Hebrew and Greek.

The third had a strong preference for the Revised Standard Version because, as he put it, "it speaks the language of our day and is much more understandable."

The fourth minister, not quite ready to express a preference, remained silent for a moment. But when he was pressed for his opinion, he surprised his colleagues with the simple statement: "I like my mother's translation best."

He didn't mean, of course, to express an indifference toward the respective merits of the various versions his friends were discussing, but he *did* want to make an important point.

It is possible for learned men to translate the original languages of the Bible into our modern idiom — without ever translating its teachings into practice. It was this latter art that his mother had mastered.

By her noble Christian life she had translated the Scriptures into something which he could read already as a child. Her love, her patience, her gentleness — these were her "translations" of the great Scriptural injunctions which she wanted to pass on to her children.

In that sense, each of us is a translator of the Bible. By our consistent Christian life we can "translate" its message to many who will never take the time to read the written Word. Whether we like it or not, *we* are the only Bibles which many people will read. Are we reliable "translations"?

In a very real sense, the Savior was asking each of us to be a relayer of God's message to man when He said: "Let your light so shine before men that they may see your good works and glorify your Father which is in heaven" (Matt. 5:16). Are we relaying — are we "translating" — His message?

God's Go-Between

During the First World War a French officer fell wounded in front of the French trenches. The enemy's shrapnel was bursting all around him as he lay there entirely unprotected.

Seeing the officer's danger, a private crawled out of the trench, dressed his wounds as best he could, and, lying down beside him, whispered in his ear:

"Do not fear! I am between you and the shells. They must hit me first."

What a beautiful picture of Him who, on Calvary's cross, placed Himself between us and the thunderbolts of God's justice. As our Savior hung there on that instrument of torture, it was as if He were saying to you and to me:

"Do not fear! I am between you and the strokes of divine justice. They must hit Me first."

Jesus is the eternal Go-between. He is the Mediator between God and men. As the Scriptures tell us: "There is one God and one Mediator between God and men, the Man Christ Jesus." (1 Tim. 2:5)

By His sinless life and by His holy, innocent suffering and death in the sinner's stead He has taken His place between me and the stern demands of God's consuming justice.

And now I need not fear. For *He* was wounded for *my* transgressions, *He* was bruised for *my* iniquities, the chastisement that brought about *my* peace was upon *Him,* and by His stripes *I* am healed. (Is. 53:5)

"Do not fear! I am between you and the shells. They must hit me first." What a glorious assurance — when we hear these words on the lips of our divine Redeemer, translated into their spiritual significance! What a wonderful comfort!

With such a Savior at our side there is nothing in life or in death that can harm us. At the dawn of each new day and at the setting of each sun, we can lift our eyes to Him and pray with confident assurance:

> Cover my defenseless head
> With the shadow of Thy wing.

The Place for Burdens

An elderly woman was the only passenger in the express elevator as it left the downstairs lobby and headed for the twentieth floor.

It was late afternoon, and it was evident that she was weary and exhausted from the heat of the day. She stood alone in the center of the elevator, her shoulders drooping with the weight of the two heavy bundles she was carrying — one in each hand.

The operator, a pleasant young lady, turned to the older woman and said: "You can put your bundles down, madam. The elevator will carry them."

Somewhat sheepishly, but nevertheless gratefully and with an audible sigh of relief, the elderly woman dropped her two bundles to the floor — and let the elevator carry them.

What a picture of many a Christian — and the way he carries his burdens! He believes with all his heart that "underneath are the everlasting arms," but he prefers to carry his burdens with his own.

The psalmist tells us: "Cast thy burden upon the *Lord*, and He shall sustain thee" (Ps. 55:22). Peter admonishes: "Casting all your care upon *Him,* for He careth for you" (1 Peter 5:7). And Moses reminds us: "The eternal God is thy Refuge, and underneath are the everlasting arms." (Deut. 33:27)

Surely, the omnipotent power which sustains us and which carries us from day to day will be able to carry our burdens also. Through Christ and His sacrificial death upon the cross we have learned that the omnipotent God is the God of love and infinite compassion. Should we be afraid to cast our burdens on such a God?

The elevator was strong enough to carry the elderly woman *and* her bundles — whether they were in her arms or on the floor. And the God of heaven is strong enough to carry us *and* our burdens — whether we insist on carrying them ourselves or have learned the art of casting them on Him.

Remember: it was to the burden bearers that the omnipotent Son of Heaven once said: "Come unto Me, all ye that labor and are heavy laden, and I will give you rest" (Matt. 11:28). Give Him your burdens! In exchange He will give you rest!

A Birthday Gift for Daddy

Aunt Martha was visiting at the home of her little niece Jodie. When Jodie's father left the living room, the little girl whispered to her aunt that she was going to give her daddy a pair of slippers for his birthday.

"Oh?" replied Aunt Martha. "And where are you going to get the money to buy them?"

Without a moment's hesitation, Jodie answered, with eyes big as saucers: "My daddy will give me the money."

Aunt Martha smiled indulgently as she thought of Jodie's father paying for his own birthday present. And she knew that he would love his daughter for the gift, even though the money that bought it was his own.

For the simple fact of the matter was that Jodie didn't own a thing that her father hadn't given her. Even the gifts which her loving heart prompted her to give him had to be paid for with *his* money!

How true that is of all of us — in our relationship to our heavenly Father! What can we possibly give Him that wasn't His before it was ours?

"The silver is Mine, and the gold is Mine," He says (Hag. 2:8). "Every beast of the forest is Mine, and the cattle upon a thousand hills" (Ps. 50:10). The whole creation is the Lord's.

Indeed, we ourselves are *His!* To each of us He says: "Fear not, for I have redeemed thee. I have called thee by thy name. Thou art *Mine!*" (Is. 43:1). The Bible makes it very clear that we are not our own. We are bought with a price — the blood of the Son of God Himself. (1 Cor. 6:19, 20)

Surely, if we and all that we have belong to Him, we can give Him nothing that is ours. We can give Him only what is His.

Like little Jodie, we can do no more than return *His* bounty as a token of our love. And like little Jodie's father, He has promised to love us for the spirit in which we give.

> We give Thee but Thine own,
> Whate'er the gift may be;
> All that we have is Thine alone,
> A trust, O Lord, from Thee.

Held by His Hand

On a cold wintry day, when the sidewalks were covered with ice, a pastor and his little boy were on their way to church. It was the first time three-year-old Bobby was wearing his new overcoat in which there were deep pockets.

As they approached a slippery place, the father said: "You had better let me hold your hand." But the boy's hands were snug in his pockets, and he kept them there — until he *slipped* and *fell!*

Somewhat humbled by this experience, he raised himself and said: "I'll hold your hand, Daddy." And he reached up and took his father's hand in a feeble grasp.

Soon they came to another slippery place — and down he went, for his tiny fingers had not been able to grip his father's hand with strength.

Once more they resumed their walk, but after a moment's reflection Bobby looked up into his father's face and said with childlike confidence: *"YOU* hold *MY* hand, Daddy." And as they went safely on their way, it was the *father's* hand that kept the boy from further danger.

How often, when *we* have come to slippery places, have we had to learn that it was not *our* hold upon God, but *His* hold upon *us* that kept our feet from stumbling! The Bible tells us: "Ye are kept by the power of God through faith unto salvation" (1 Peter 1:5). It is

He, not we; and it is His power, not ours, that does the keeping.

What a comfort, as we set out on the precarious path of each new day, to know that it is His hand that will lead us and will hold us every step of the way. For we know that the hand that is stretched from heaven to help us is the hand that was pierced to save us from our ruin.

In His hands we are safe. He knows us and He loves us. And we follow Him. And He gives us eternal life. And no man shall pluck us from His hands. (John 10:27-29)

What an appropriate prayer at the opening of each new day: "YOU hold MY hand, Lord Jesus!"

> I am trusting Thee, Lord Jesus,
> Trusting only Thee;
> Trusting Thee for full salvation,
> Great and free.
>
> I am trusting Thee, Lord Jesus;
> Never let me fall;
> I am trusting Thee forever
> — And for all!

He Got Straight A's

The pastor was visiting in little Johnnie's home. He was conducting a home-to-home visitation — in an effort to strengthen the spiritual life of the families in his parish.

After having discussed spiritual matters with Johnnie's parents, the pastor turned to little Johnnie.

"And do you say your prayers every day?" "Yes, sir!" "Before and after meals?" "Yes, sir!" "And when you go to bed, and when you get up in the mornings?" "Yes, sir!"

"And do you pray the Lord to bless you in your school work?"

"Oh, no, sir! I get straight A's!"

Somehow it didn't seem important to little Johnnie that he pray for the Lord's blessing upon his studies — for, after all, how much better could he do than get a perfect report card!

We may smile for a moment, but, having smiled, let us take a serious look at ourselves. How often have we become remiss in our prayers just because we were "getting straight A's"?

When things are going wrong, when difficulties loom large on every side, when problems become unsolvable, when the deep questions of life go begging for an answer — *then* prayer seems a very natural (yes, a very needed) exercise.

But when life becomes for us a succession of beautiful mornings, when it seems that "everything's going our way," when good fortune smiles on us at every turn — *then* prayer, somehow, seems just a bit superfluous.

What every one of us needs to remember is that prayer is *never* superfluous — even when we are "getting straight A's." For who is it that is giving us those A's — if not the God from whom *all* blessings flow?

Prayer, we must remember, is not merely a matter of asking — it is also a matter of thanking, of praising, of communing, of confiding.

Who could ever run out of things for which to thank and praise his Lord? Or who could ever run out of things about which to speak to God?

Little Johnnie knew better, of course. And so do we. But do we always *act* according to our knowledge?

Footprints of the Stars

Our point of vantage to-night is a French window in a Hollywood hotel, over-looking Hollywood Boulevard. From our room on the twelfth floor we are looking down at the world-famous Grauman's Chinese theater, which is just across the street.

We have looked down at this brilliantly lit Mecca of the entertainment world a hundred times before — always with a vague feeling of sadness and regret. But perhaps never with the poignancy which has touched our heart tonight.

Day after day, year after year, morning, noon, and night, a steady parade of curious tourists lingers in front of the theater to look at the "footprints of the stars." Engraved in a vast expanse of concrete are the footprints, handprints, legprints, and autographs of well-known movie celebrities — many of whom are no longer among the living.

Children of all ages — under seven and over seventy — delight in putting their feet into the footprints of the stars so that they can tell their friends back home: "I walked in the very same spot where Jean Harlow and John Gilbert walked!"

Perhaps there is a *special* reason for our melancholy mood as we look down at that endless parade tonight. We have just laid our Bible aside after reading God's *own* tablet, in which are engraved the footprints of *His* stars: Hebrews, chapter eleven.

"By faith, Abel. . . . By faith, Enoch. . . . By faith, Noah, Abraham, Isaac, Jacob, Joseph, Moses. . . ." These are the men whose footprints God has asked us to study and to follow — the footprints of *faith* and love and duty.

Long after the footprints in the concrete across the street have crumbled into dust, the footprints of the faithful will continue to show the way to generations yet unborn.

Thank God that — far from the glitter and the glamour of this transitory world — there is a vast un-numbered host of those who are trying, with God's help, to match their footsteps to the paths His faithful followed.

"You'll Know Where to Find Me"

An elderly pastor lay critically ill. In the opinion of his doctor he could live only a few days more.

His wife put through a long-distance call to their son, who was also a pastor and who served a congregation in a small town three hundred miles away.

Within a few hours the son was at his father's bedside, and the two men prayed together.

Saturday came, and there was no change in the elderly man's condition. Calling his son to his bedside, he spoke in a weak and faltering voice:

"Go back to your congregation, son, and preach tomorrow. If I should slip away while you are gone, you'll know where to find me."

"You'll know where to find me!"

What a wonderful thing, when a father can speak thus to his children!

What a wonderful thing at the sunset of life, to know just where we will be at eternity's dawn — in our Father's house, in the company of our Savior, who has gone ahead to prepare a place for us.

And what a wonderful thing for a father who is taking leave of his children to know that they, *too,* have learned the way to the place where he is going; and that they, too, by God's grace, will share a mansion in the Father's house above.

"You'll know where to find me!"

Let those of us who are fathers and mothers ask ourselves: have we arrived at that spiritual certainty which will enable us, at the end of life, to say: "I *know* where I am going?"

And have we passed on this knowledge and this faith to our children so that we can say confidently to them: *"You'll* know where to find me"?

We can do *both* if, by God's grace, we root our faith — our own and that of our children — firmly in Him who died for us and who even now is awaiting our arrival in His Father's house above.

Too Poor to Pay

In a Scottish village lived a doctor noted for his generosity. After his death, when his books were examined, quite a few of his accounts were found to have a line written across them in red ink: "Forgiven. Too poor to pay."

Some months after his death his widow, being somewhat less generous, insisted that these bills *must* be paid, and immediately instituted court proceedings.

After examining one bill after another, the lawyer asked the widow: "Is this your husband's handwriting in red?" She admitted that it was.

"Then," said the lawyer, "there is no tribunal in the land that can obtain the money for you. If your husband has written 'forgiven,' these debts are forgiven."

Similarly God has written "forgiven" over the record of sin of every member of the human family. The Bible says: "God was in Christ, reconciling the world unto Himself, not imputing [that is, not charging] their trespasses unto them." (2 Cor. 5:19)

Again it says: "Having forgiven you all trespasses . . . blotting out the handwriting . . . that was against us . . . nailing it to His cross." (Col. 2:13, 14)

Indeed, that is the central purpose of the entire Bible: to tell us that, when Christ died on the cross for our sins, His Father wrote "forgiven" across our guilty record.

[144]

Our conscience, our human reason, and the unbelieving world may challenge that assertion. They may do their best to convince us that the debt of our iniquity has *not* been canceled.

Be that as it may. We have the word of Him to whom the debt was owed and who alone has the power to forgive. And He has written His assurance in crimson letters — "in whom we have redemption through His *blood,* the forgiveness of sins, according to the riches of His grace." (Eph. 1:7)

The eternal Son of God Himself paid for those who, because of their spiritual poverty, were "too poor to pay."

"Lucky Boy!"

It was only a few Christmases ago that a distressed mother, who could no longer care for her infant son, gave him to a state agency for adoption.

Little did she or anyone else know that within a few weeks the child would be adopted by a wealthy couple in California — a couple whose annual income ranges between $1,000,000 and $1,500,000.

After all requirements had been met and all the necessary documents had been signed, the bouncing boy of fifteen months was declared the legal heir of a fortune which came close to $20,000,000.

"Lucky boy!" At least, we hope that his sudden good fortune will prove to be a blessing.

What this wealthy couple did for this helpless infant just two or three Christmases ago, God did for *you* and *me* on the very first Christmas — only in a much higher sense. Through the miracle of Christmas God made it possible for us to be adopted into His family and to be made heirs of eternal treasures, indescribable and immeasurable.

The Bible tells us that by nature we were *not* God's children — but rather "the children of wrath, even as others" (Eph. 2:3). But it also tells us that on the first Christmas, "when the fullness of the time was come, God sent forth His Son, made of a woman, made under the Law, to redeem them that were under the Law, *that we might receive the adoption of sons. . . .* Wherefore thou art no more a servant, but a son; and if a son, then an heir of God through Christ." (Gal. 4:4, 5, 7)

Because of what happened on that first Christmas you and I are sons and daughters of God. Heirs of God — through Christ! That is the message of Christmas.

And having been adopted into the family of God, we have come into possession of the treasures of heaven: forgiveness of sins; fellowship with God; life, full, free, abundant, and eternal.

Because Christ became a Son of earth, you today are a son of heaven! "Lucky boy" — you and I!

> We are rich, for He was poor;
> Is not this a wonder?
> Therefore praise God evermore,
> Here on earth and yonder!

She Wasn't Lost

A father and his six-year-old daughter were walking through the downtown streets of the city to which they had recently moved.

With almost no conversation between them, they turned corner after corner, taking in the sights of the unfamiliar streets.

After some time the little girl looked up and said: "Daddy, are *you* lost?" There was an anxious look on her face, which did not escape her father. But instead of answering her directly, he tightened his grip on her little hand and asked: "Are *you* lost?"

A smile brightened her face. "Oh, no," she said quickly, "I'm with *you*, Daddy!" And with that her fears were gone.

How could she be lost as long as she was with her father — or as long as he was with her?

And how can you and I be lost as long as we know that our heavenly Father is with us — and we are with Him?

As we turn the corner of each new day, each new week, or each new year and look down the long and unfamiliar road which lies ahead, we are likely to shrink from the uninviting prospect. There are so many uncertainties, so many problems, so many pitfalls, so many dangers!

Sometimes, indeed, as we stand falteringly in the present and look trembling into the future, we feel that we are *lost* — alone in an unfriendly world — unequal to the task of carrying on.

Indeed, sometimes we feel that *God and we* are lost in a world which is upside down, in a world in which everything is going topsy-turvy. . . .

As we stand upon the threshold of each new day, at each new turn on the pathway of life let us remind ourselves that our heavenly Father is never lost — and that we His children, who have come to Him by faith in Jesus Christ, our Savior, are forever safe within His keeping.

With our hand in His, let us walk courageously into today, tomorrow — into the many tomorrows which still lie before us. For each tomorrow belongs to Him.

What God Looks Like

It happened during a vacation Bible school. The first-grade pupils were asked to draw a picture of anything or anyone they chose. Fifteen minutes would be devoted to what the children called their "drawing period."

After a minute or two Mary Jane looked over the shoulder of little Margie, who sat in front of her, and eagerly asked: "What are *you* going to draw?"

With the nonchalance of which a six-year-old is frequently capable, Margie looked back over her shoulder and said: "I'm drawing a picture of God."

Assuming an air of superior wisdom, Mary Jane retorted: "Aw — *nobody* knows what God looks like!"

Little Margie couldn't quite agree. After biting her pencil a moment, she replied with sudden determination: "They will when *I'M* through!"

We don't know what Margie finally put on her paper, but we like the idea she had in her heart. She was determined that when she was through, the children around her would have a better idea of what God is like.

And, come to think of it, isn't that the purpose of *every* Christian life — to show the people around us what God is like?

St. Paul says that we are the epistles of Christ, "written not with ink but with the Spirit of the living God;

not on tablets of stone but on tablets of human hearts."
(2 Cor. 3:3 RSV)

One of the chief purposes of our being in this world
is to show people, by word and deed, what God is like.
We are to communicate to them the vital facts of divine
revelation: that God is holy, just, and righteous; but
also merciful, kind, and gracious through Jesus Christ,
His Son.

We may not have little Margie's pencil in our hand,
but we do have a *life* in our hands. And with that life
we are to show the world "what God is like."

A Star in God's Window

It was an early spring evening during the First World War. A father and his four-year-old son were taking a leisurely stroll through a residential neighborhood.

As they walked by a darkened home, little Bobby noticed a service flag in the window — with a gold star on a field of white.

"What kind of flag is that, Daddy?" the lad inquired as he tugged at his father's coat sleeve.

"That star, Bobby, means that the people in that home have lost a son in the war. Their boy died fighting for our freedom."

His question answered, little Bobby was satisfied. Quietly he walked by his father's side as they continued down the street.

A few moments later, 'way off in the distance, over the chimney of a house almost a block away, a twinkling star appeared in the sky. It was the first star of the evening, and it engaged the attention of the wondering lad as he shuffled along the sidewalk.

Suddenly, as if struck by a new and momentous thought, the boy looked up at his father and asked: "Daddy, did *GOD* lose a son in the war?"

Momentarily at a loss for words, the father looked down at his son, laid a tender hand on his head, and smiled.

"Yes, Bobby, God *did* give up His Son. His Son died on a cross, so that you and I and Mother — and *all* people — might be free.

"I hope that as long as you live, you will always think of God's Son and what He did for us, every time you look at the gold star up there in His window."

His question answered, little Bobby was satisfied again. And he walked quietly by his father's side as they continued on their homeward way.

And as the older man looked at the golden star shimmering in the distance, he thought within himself:

"God so loved the world that He gave His only-begotten Son, that whosoever believeth in Him should not perish but have everlasting life." (John 3:16)

". . . But I'm Your Father!"

Recently the son of a wealthy and respected citizen became guilty of a serious offense. Not only did his behavior bring disgrace upon the family name, but it involved the family in a lawsuit which threatened its comfortable fortune.

The young man was worried about the attitude his father would take. Would he disown him? Would he give vent to his righteous anger? Would he turn on him in fury and berate him for his wicked folly?

When the remorseful young man was finally confronted by his father, the older man did nothing of the sort.

"Son," he said, "I do not condone the terrible thing you've done. I condemn it with every fiber of my being. But I'm your *father*. And I'm determined to suffer this whole thing through with you."

In a similar but immeasurably higher sense the God of heaven took pity on His erring sons and daughters. He condemned their transgressions, and He loathed their sins. But in His mercy He determined to identify Himself with the sufferings which resulted from their wickedness.

He decided to suffer not only *with* His wayward children but also, and pre-eminently, *FOR* them. That is the central message of the Christian Gospel.

[154]

"God commendeth His love toward us in that, while we were yet sinners, Christ died for us." (Rom. 5:8)

Who showed His love toward us? God! Who died for us? Christ! There may be much mystery tied up in that sentence, but there can be no doubt about its essential message: the God of heaven took pity on His erring children and, through Jesus Christ, His Son, He suffered in their stead.

God entered into human suffering through His own beloved Son in order that He might "see us through" — in order that our penalty might be paid and we might be free forever.

It is of Christ, the Son of God, that the Scriptures say: "He was wounded for our transgressions . . . and with His stripes we are healed." (Is. 53:4, 5)

God did not *have* to do this for us. But God is our Father! And so He did!

Last Year's Sermons—Where Are They?

The pastor and his wife were working in his study. They were busy packing books and papers, preparatory to moving into the new parsonage.

Ever since he had entered the ministry, the pastor had carefully wrapped his sermon manuscripts into separate bundles — a bundle for each year — and had written the year on an index card which he inserted at the top of each package.

In his hands he held his sermons for 1956, 1957, and 1958. But the sermons for 1959 were missing. And so, in a worried tone, he inquired of his wife: "Last year's sermons — where are they?"

Half humorously, half philosophically, his devoted spouse replied: *"I've often wondered!"*

She had often wondered what became of a sermon a year after it was preached. Not that she doubted the effective power of the Gospel, but in her weaker moments she had her misgivings about the permanent effect of many a sermon her husband had preached.

Perhaps all of us have wondered at some time or other what has become of last year's sermons — the sermons we've heard and long forgotten. Where are they? . . .

Where is last year's sunshine — the warm rays that fell gently on fields and gardens? In one sense, they are gone. But in another they are here. They have gone into grains and fruits and vegetables which still sustain your life and mine.

In the food we eat today the sunshine of yesterday is still carrying out God's purposes.

And where are last year's raindrops? They, too, have long been forgotten. But they accomplished, and continue to accomplish, God's purposes. They did their refreshing work.

Had they not come in due season — *last year* — you and I would be the poorer *this year*. Thank God for last year's raindrops!

And where are last year's sermons? They, too, have come and gone. But in the providence of God they accomplished, and they *continue* to accomplish, His own designs.

God Himself has said: "So shall My Word be . . . It shall not return to Me void, but it shall accomplish that which I please, and it shall prosper in the thing whereto I sent it." (Is. 55:11)

That applies not only to this year's sermons — but also to last year's.

The Congregation Was Perfectly Behaved

The church service was one of the most orderly we have ever attended.

The worshipers sat in their pews — erect, wide awake, and alert, eager to participate in every part of the service.

They sang each hymn with fervor, spoke each prayer precisely and with evident conviction. And when the preacher ascended the pulpit and announced his text, every eye in the vast assembly was riveted on the man who was about to bring a message from God's Word.

There was no squirming in the pews, no whispered conversation, no yawning, no searching of purses for chewing gum or cough drops, no craning of necks, no looking back to see if Aunt Jane or Uncle Jim were sitting in the balcony.

In fact, if we had not known the *reason* for this almost perfect decorum, we would not have believed our eyes — or ears.

But we knew the reason!

In the back of the church, as well as in the balcony and in the far corners of the transept, were huge television cameras; and at strategic points throughout the sanctuary there were well-concealed microphones.

These electronic eyes and ears were trained on every worshiper (at least, so it seemed), recording his every act and preserving it permanently on film. For just six hours later the entire worship service would be shown to countless television viewers by means of a kinescope.

With these almost omnipresent eyes and ears before him and behind him, every worshiper was on his best behavior.

We couldn't keep from thinking: how different the average worship service would be if each of us were as keenly aware of the invisible eye and ear of the Almighty, which are just as surely present every Sunday morning!

"Thou, God, seest me" (Gen. 16:13). He sees our every act and hears our every thought. Let us remember that when we go to church next Sunday.

None of Our Business?

It happened during the depression of the early thirties. A mother and her four-year-old daughter were walking along a downtown street, when they became aware of a shabbily dressed man standing at a corner, holding out his ragged cap and asking for a "few pennies."

"O Mamma," said the little girl as she tugged on her mother's coat sleeve, "let's help him." The mother reached for her daughter's hand and, hurrying her on her way, said: "Come along, dear; it isn't any of our business."

Not quite sure that she had understood her mother's reasoning, the little girl nevertheless obeyed. Before long she forgot the man at the corner, as her mind became occupied with the toys and doll buggies in the store windows.

But that night, after she had prayed her bedtime prayers, she paused for a moment and then in childlike innocence added: "And, please God, bless that poor man on the corner." At that moment her eyes met those of her mother, and she remembered what her mother had said that afternoon. And so she quickly added: "Oh, no, God. He really isn't any of our business, *is* he?" . . .

We don't know what the mother thought or said at that humiliating moment, but we are sure she did some speaking to God herself — after the lights were out.

Yes, the poor of this world *are* God's business. And they are *our* business, too. The millions of people all over the world who are ill fed, ill clad, ill housed — the refugees, the displaced, the helpless, and the hopeless — all of them are God's business, *and ours*.

The Lord admonishes His people: "Let us not grow weary in well-doing, for in due season we shall reap, if we do not lose heart. So then, as we have opportunity, let us do good to all men, and especially to those who are of the household of faith." (Gal. 6:9, 10 RSV)

Well-doing, after all, *is* the Christian's business!

When the Signs Got Mixed

Suburban residents of a Midwest town were half amused, half confused, when they approached an intersection one morning and found more than a dozen traffic signs — all giving contradictory directions.

They learned later that a traffic crew had deposited the signs at that corner temporarily, awaiting the arrival of another truck which would carry them to their proper destination.

Meanwhile the miscellaneous assortment of signs shouted to all approaching motorists: "No Left Turn!" "Turn Left!" "Stop!" "Turn Right!"

Not so amusing, but infinitely more confusing, is the plight of many a person today who is looking for the "right road" to eternal salvation. With more than 200 brands of religion in the United States alone, he doesn't know which "sign" to follow.

But amid this confusion of directions there *is* a "sign" which we can follow with absolute assurance. Our Savior says: "I am the Way, the Truth, and the Life. No man cometh to the Father but by Me." (John 14:6)

The one and only road that leads to heaven, according to the Bible, is the road of repentance for sin and personal faith in Jesus as our Savior.

"Neither is there salvation in any other; for there is none other name under heaven given among men whereby we must be saved." (Acts 4:12)

The road to heaven always leads across Mount Calvary. Any sign that promises heaven by a different road is false. Are we on the Calvary road?

When the Lights Go Out

It was a late autumn evening during the Second World War. The entire city of London lay in inky darkness due to a strictly enforced blackout.

After the evening meal was over, a London father invited his eight-year-old son to take a walk with him — to get a breath of fresh air.

Together they walked down the darkened streets until the lad suddenly remarked, as if he had made an unexpected discovery, "Daddy, we never saw the stars over the city until the lights went out!"

How true! True not only of the dark nights over London, but true also of the dark nights which again and again settle down over our individual lives. How often have we had good reason to lift our eyes heavenward and exclaim: "O Father, I never saw Your stars over my little life until the lights went out!"

Sometimes it takes the darkness of sadness or sickness, loneliness or bereavement, disappointment or disillusionment, anxiety or despair to bring out the radiance and the brilliance of God's firmament of Gospel promises.

How often in the silent darkness of some depressing sorrow have we been cheered by the warm light of those promises, shimmering like stars in the heavens: "Lo, I am with you always." "Fear not, I am with thee."

[164]

"I shall never leave thee nor forsake thee." "I have redeemed thee. Thou art Mine."

In the broad daylight of prosperity, when everything is going our way, when health, wealth, and happy friendships cheer our way — our eyes sometimes lose sight of these promises.

But when the lights are out, when health and wealth and friends are gone, these promises are still there — eternal in the Gospel firmament. Men and fortunes may change, but God's assurances go on forever. They are like the stars in His heavens.

Whether the lights of our life are on or out, may our eyes be fixed on His unchanging Gospel. It is *there* — in darkness and in light.

Taller Than Before

A traveling salesman was "making conversation" with an eccentric farmer whom he hoped to interest in some new equipment for his farm.

Seated on the veranda with his not too promising prospect, the salesman noticed a rough drawing of what looked like a barn — lying on a nearby chair.

Picking it up and studying it for a moment, he asked the farmer if this was a drawing of the new barn he intended to build.

"Yep," replied the farmer.

Puzzled, the salesman inquired: "Why so wide and so long and only about *half as tall* as a normal barn should be?"

The farmer had his own reasons for drawing his plan as he did. But being in no mood to prolong what was turning out to be a boring conversation, he replied jokingly: "So that when it gets blown over, it'll be higher than it was before!"

We may not fully appreciate the farmer's sense of humor, but we can extract a bit of wisdom from his reply. How important, in planning our life, that we build it "so that when it gets blown over, it will be higher than it was before!"

Lives *can* be built that way — if they are built on the sure foundation of the Christian Gospel — if their roots are sunk deep into the immovable assurances which God has given us in Christ.

He whose strength is made perfect in our weakness has a way of making lives stand taller after they have been blown over.

The pages of history are filled with the triumphs of Christian people whose lives were blown topsy-turvy by the winds of adversity, but who went on to splendid achievements — not in spite of, *but because of,* the very winds which seemed to spell calamity. Their lives were taller, because they had been blown over!

Have our lives been thus built? Are they standing firm and four-square on the immovable foundation of God — the foundation which He has provided us in Christ?

"Mother, Are You Worrying?"

Mother, are you worrying?"

Mrs. Carter was startled by this unexpected question. Standing in the doorway to the living room was five-year-old Eddie, clad in his pajamas and wearing a look on his face as though he hadn't a friend in the world.

She had put little Eddie to bed more than an hour ago and thought that he had long since drifted off to sleep. But there he was in the doorway, wide awake and evidently troubled, eager to have an answer to his question.

At a loss at first to explain what the boy meant by his unusual query, she was soon to find out what was troubling his little heart. When she had put him to bed earlier that evening, he had confided to her one of his big little problems, for which a solution had to be found before tomorrow morning.

In true mother fashion she had assured him that everything would be all right. And as she tucked him in and kissed him good night, she had said: "Now, you just go to sleep — *and let Mother worry about that.*"

An hour had passed, and the lad wasn't sure that his mother was keeping her promise. Was she *really* "worrying about that"? Might she have forgotten? He had to make sure. And so at length he crawled out of bed, went slowly down the stairs, peeked into the living room, and asked timidly:

"Mother, are you worrying?"

We may smile at little Eddie, but aren't we all very much like him? The Bible invites us again and again to cast all our cares, our worries and anxieties, upon the Lord. And He assures us that He will "care *for* us." (1 Peter 5:7)

It is because we are spiritual children that we find it impossible to take God at His word. How often have we stayed awake at night because we weren't sure that God would keep His promise to care for us — tonight, tomorrow?

Let us never forget that God's "good night" to the praying Christian is very similar to that of Eddie's mother: "Now, you just go to sleep — and let *Me* worry about those problems."

If You Want to See the Christ Child . . .

Christmas 1906 was going to be a cheerless day for the Lars Ericksons.

In poor health and out of work, Lars had reached the point where he didn't care if Christmas ever came or not. Depressed and irritable, he made poor company for his faithful wife, Anna, and his five-year-old daughter, Greta, as they sat around their coal stove on a cold December evening.

Little Greta, seated on the floor, was busily at work with her scissors, cardboard, and paste, constructing a crude little "manger set," which she had spread out on the carpet in front of the stove.

"How do you like it, Daddy?" she asked.

"Fine," he answered disinterestedly.

"And how do you like the *manger?*"

"I can't see it from here," was his grumpy reply.

Looking up into her daddy's face, she said, with a wisdom of which she herself was not aware: "If you want to see the Christ Child, you'll have to get down on your knees."

How true! True not only of Lars Erickson, but also of you and me. If we want to see the Christ Child, we'll have to get down on our knees.

If there were a special Beatitude for Christmas, it would read: "Blessed are the poor in spirit, for they shall behold the Infant Christ."

Blessed are they who come to the manger meek and lowly, for they shall see the "Wonderful, the Counselor, the Mighty God, the Everlasting Father, the Prince of Peace." (Is. 9:6)

As we travel in spirit to Bethlehem's manger, let us make sure that we approach the Christ Child in true humility. If we will bring Him our weakness, He will give us strength. If we will bring Him our sorrows, He will give us joy. Above all, if we will bring Him our *sins,* He will give us pardon, full and free.

It has always been true, and it will remain *forever* true, that "if you want to see the Christ Child, you will have to get down on your knees."

The Clock That Stopped

A little clock in a jeweler's window stopped one day for only half an hour. The hands stood still at twenty minutes after eight.

School children on their way to school, noticing the time, stopped to play as they sauntered along the sidewalk; people on their way to work, when they saw the clock, slowed their pace; and a man, hurrying to catch a train, slackened his gait when he saw that he still had plenty of time.

But the children were late for school, the older people were late for work, and the businessman missed his train — all because one little clock had stopped! Never had these people realized how much they had depended on that little clock in the jeweler's window — until for the first time in their lives it had led them astray.

In a sense, everyone who professes the Christian faith and claims to lead a Christian life is very much like that little clock. People all around us are, consciously or unconsciously, being influenced by what we say and do.

If we permit our Christianity to "stop" for just a little while, if by careless speech or improper conduct we set a bad example, we are likely to lead our fellow men astray, just as surely as did the timepiece in the jeweler's window.

It is wrong to assume, even for a moment, that our lives, just because they are little, do not count; that our actions are unimportant; that our influence is insignificant. In a sense more real than many of us suppose, God has placed every Christian into the world to "tell the time" — to influence our fellow men as they journey toward eternity.

"You are the light of the world" (Matt. 5:14), says Christ. You are an instrument in His hands to bring others to Him and to heaven. How important, then, that those who read our lives may be led into paths of *truth*.

A stopped clock tells the truth only twice a day. All the rest of its life — is a lie! God has no use for "stopped clocks" in His kingdom.

A Debt of Love

A soldier in the South Pacific lay unconscious for days in an improvised hospital behind the lines.

He was critically in need of blood, but there was no plasma to be had. A sergeant, with whom he had not been on very friendly terms, volunteered to give some of his own blood to save the life of the young GI.

When the wounded man came to a few days later, he was told that he owed his life to the sergeant whom he had previously regarded with unconcealed disdain.

He wanted to thank his benefactor, but the sergeant had been transferred to another island that very morning, and it was not at all certain that the two men would ever meet again.

"I'll find him, if it's the last thing I do," said the young soldier. "I owe my life to him, and I won't rest until I've thanked him!"

The way that young GI felt toward the man whose blood had spelled the difference between life and death for him, is the way the Christian feels toward Jesus Christ, his Savior. "I owe my life to Him, and I won't rest until I've thanked Him!"

There is a divine restlessness that seizes the heart of every person who is keenly aware of the price of his redemption. He cannot be at ease until he has poured out the last full measure of devotion to Him who has redeemed his soul from death.

In a very real sense, the whole Christian life is the response of gratitude on the part of the redeemed, addressed to the Redeemer. Every deed of love, every kindness, every conscious act of Christian virtue is, in a very real sense, a thank-You to the One who paid the price of our salvation.

The apostle Paul put it eloquently when he wrote to the Galatians: "I am crucified with Christ; nevertheless I live; yet not I, but Christ liveth in me. And the life which I now live in the flesh I live by the faith of the Son of God, who loved me *and gave Himself for me.*" (Gal. 2:20)

Surely, Paul could have voiced his devotion to Christ in the words of the young soldier: "I owe my life to Him, and I won't rest until I've thanked Him."

Can we say the same?

He Rose Again!

A well-dressed gentleman was standing in front of the display window of an art store, looking at a painting of the Crucifixion.

As he stood there, a little boy in dirty blue jeans and a tattered sweat shirt walked up and stood beside him — also intent on the painting.

Pointing to the picture, the man asked the lad: "Do you know who that is, hanging on the cross?" "Oh, yes, sir," came the quick response, "that's the Savior."

And as he spoke, the small boy's eyes showed surprise and pity at the ignorance of the unknown gentleman. Then, after a pause, with an evident desire to enlighten the man, he added: "Them's the soldiers, the Roman soldiers," and with a long sigh, "that lady crying there is His mother."

After another brief moment of silence he added: "They killed Him, mister. They *killed* Him."

Together they studied the painting in silence until finally the man tousled the boy's hair affectionately and walked away, disappearing into the crowd.

He had turned a corner and walked a half block when suddenly he heard the shrill voice of the lad, who was making his way through the crowd: "Hey, mister! Mister!"

He turned and waited for the eager youngster to catch up with him. Almost out of breath, the lad panted his excited information: "I wanted to tell you, He rose again! He rose again!"

What a message!

Whether the little boy realized it or not, he would never again in all his life deliver a message of greater importance. No sputnik, no satellite, no landing on the moon, no interplanetary travel would ever provide a more important headline than the one his youthful lips had just formed: "Hey, mister! He rose again!"

God's greatest message to man is the message of His Son, whether it be formed on the lips of an eager youngster — "They killed Him! He rose again!" — or by the pen of His inspired apostle: "He was delivered for our offenses and was raised again for our justification!" (Rom. 4:25)

Unforgivable?

A distressed mother came to her pastor with the excited confession: "Pastor, I have committed the unpardonable sin!"

The kind and wise clergyman gave no sign of surprise or alarm but simply asked her in a restrained and quiet voice: "And are you sorry for it?"

"Yes, Pastor, *dreadfully* sorry!" was her anguished reply.

"Then you have committed nothing that cannot be forgiven. There is no sin, no matter how great, that cannot be forgiven through sincere repentance and trusting faith in Jesus, our Redeemer."

Behind that simple, reassuring answer of her pastor lay the full authority of Scripture. In a very real sense it was not he but God who was speaking to her troubled conscience.

That is the supreme glory and comfort of the Christian Gospel. The disease cannot spread farther than the cure. "Where sin abounded, grace did much more abound." (Rom. 5:20)

There was sufficient grace for penitent Peter, who "went out and wept bitterly" (Matt. 26:75). There was sufficient grace for anguished Paul, who cried out: "Oh, wretched man that I am!" (Rom. 7:24). There was sufficient grace for the sin-burdened publican, who smote upon his breast and said: "God, be merciful to me, a sinner!" (Luke 18:13)

And there is sufficient grace for you! All who have learned to look with terror upon their own iniquities and have learned to lift pleading eyes toward Calvary's cross for the assurance of forgiveness have found a limitless reservoir of divine grace.

No matter who you are, no matter how far you have drifted from God and His Word, no matter how great your sin, the Savior's promise is still for you: "Him that cometh to Me *I will in no wise cast out.*" (John 6:37)

I heard the voice of Jesus say,
"Come unto Me and rest;
Lay down, thou weary one, lay down
Thy head upon My breast."
I came to Jesus as I was,
Weary and worn and sad;
I found in Him a resting place,
And He has made me glad!

Familiar Darkness

Little three-year-old Linda was spending the weekend with her aunt and uncle. It was the first time she had ever been away from her daddy and mother overnight.

She had romped and played all day and had enjoyed every minute of it. Her admiring aunt had just read her a bedtime story, had listened to her prayers, tucked her snugly in bed, and kissed her good night.

As she left the room, she whispered a fond "sleep tight" and turned out the light.

Sometime later she passed the child's room again and thought she heard restrained sobbing. Opening the bedroom door, she found the little girl crying her heart out. "Why — what is it, Linda?" she asked.

"I'm afraid in the dark," the child cried. "But you always sleep in the dark at home," the aunt tried to assure her. "Yes — but that's *MY* dark," Linda sobbed.

Her "dark" was different! The "dark" in her own room held no terror for her, because she knew what was in her room *in the light*. Her doll, her teddybear, her rocking chair, her toy chest — she knew where each one was in the light, and she knew that they must still be there in the dark, surrounding her at night just as they surrounded her at day.

And so she was not afraid in HER dark!

What a striking picture of the believing child of God in *his* darkness. Each of us must live through the night of his own adversity, the night of his own sorrow, trial, and affliction. But having looked into the face of Christ, we are not afraid of *"our* dark," because in the very midst of that "dark" we are aware of the comforting presence of Him whom our eye of faith has seen so often — in darkness and in light.

And we know that He is with us in our "dark," even as He has been with us in our light, reaching out His hand to ours, speaking pardon to our souls, whispering assurance to our hearts.

In darkness and in light He has assured us: "I will never leave thee nor forsake thee." (Heb. 13:5)

For darkness and light are both alike to Him.

A Sermon on a Bus

It was a blazing-hot day in St. Louis. The temperature was high in the nineties, and we were standing on a downtown corner, bathed in perspiration, waiting for one of our city's newest air-conditioned buses.

Suddenly it turned the corner and stopped in front of us, and we lost no time in boarding it. As we stepped out of the scorching sun into the refrigerated vehicle, we were shocked and stunned by the sudden change in temperature.

For a block or two we sat miserably uncomfortable — our body quivering, our teeth chattering — debating whether or not to leave the bus. Would we be able to stand this for the forty-minute ride? Would we become ill? Would we catch our death of cold?

Eying the other passengers, we chided ourself for such cowardly thoughts and began reading the magazine which we had brought along, soon becoming absorbed in its contents.

It was perhaps ten minutes later that we laid the magazine on our lap and began daydreaming. Why were we suddenly so comfortable? What had become of the icy air? When had the change taken place? And what was it, really, that had changed — the temperature in the bus, or we?

It was not the temperature in the bus that had changed! It was we who, without being aware of it, had become comfortable in the selfsame atmosphere which only ten minutes ago we had found so "shocking." Not the air in the bus, but we had changed!

What a parable of life, we thought. How imperceptibly does the atmosphere of the world close in upon us! How gradually do we become acclimated to the allurements of worldly pleasure, and how unconsciously do we lose our sense of shock!

Many a Christian who not long ago would have shuddered at the thought or at the sight of certain sins now finds himself completely comfortable in their presence. To him it may seem that these sins have changed — that they have become less sinful in God's sight. But it is not the sins that have changed. It is *he!*

Surely each of us has every reason to be on his guard, lest, all unknown to us, the world close in upon us — and we become *comfortable* where God would have us *shocked.*

Limping at the Shepherd's Side

A traveler in Palestine joined a shepherd as he led his flock across a Palestinian hill. As they walked along and conversed leisurely, the traveler noticed one of the older sheep which walked with some difficulty — always within a short distance from the shepherd.

Curious, he asked the shepherd why it was that this sheep walked with a noticeable limp and why it was that it never ventured more than a few feet away from the shepherd.

"That sheep," explained the shepherd, "is one of the oldest in the flock. Soon after it was born, I learned that it was partially deaf. When it was a little lamb, it persisted in straying from the fold, where it could not hear my voice.

"Many was the time that I was called upon to rescue it from the brink of destruction — until finally I had to inflict that injury on its leg myself. Ever since that day the sheep has limped, but it has also stayed much closer to me for guidance and protection."

Limping at the shepherd's side! What a picture of the blessedness of the Christian cross-bearer! Limping, yes! But limping — at his Shepherd's side!

The apostle Paul had a similar "limp." He called it his thorn in the flesh. To him it was "the messenger of Satan to buffet me, lest I should be exalted above measure. For this thing I besought the Lord thrice that it might depart from me. And He said unto me: My grace is sufficient for thee; for My strength is made perfect in weakness." (2 Cor. 12:7-9)

Our Father's love may have found it necessary to wound us, to visit us with some sorrow, some bitter disappointment, some bodily affliction; but we can rest assured in the conviction: it was His *love* that did it.

If God has given us a burden that is causing us to limp, we may be sure that He wants to use that burden to draw us closer to His side.

> Beloved, "It is well!"
> Though deep and sore the smart,
> The hand that wounds knows how to bind
> And heal the broken heart.

"Of His Kingdom There Shall Be No End"

E. Stanley Jones tells how once he traveled from France to India by plane.

In the early morning he left Marseilles and stopped to refuel at Corsica. He remembered that it was from this island that Napoleon went forth to conquer the world

At noon he lunched in Naples; and as he lunched, his mind went back to the Caesars who had gone forth from this land to subdue the earth.

At nightfall he was in Greece, and in memory he went back to Alexander the Great who, starting from this ancient land of might and culture, had gone forth to be a world conqueror.

The next day he flew past Assyria on the left and Babylon on the right, lands from which mighty monarchs had gone forth to make the earth tremble.

As he flew over these countries, he said, he was struck by the fact that every one of these mighty empires, with their powerful dictators, is dead and gone. Within each empire had been the seed of its own decay and dissolution — the seed of human sin.

Only one empire, begun in the lands over which he flew, still remains. And that is the empire which had its humble beginning in the unspectacular land of Palestine — in the little town of Bethlehem.

The King who was born in a stable, cradled in straw, rejected by men, and nailed to a cross, still *reigns!*

He reigns in heaven among His holy angels. He reigns in His church — that empire which He rules by love and someday will bring victorious to His homeland. He reigns on earth by the might of His omnipotence, still governing the destinies of nations.

Napoleons, Caesars, Alexanders have come and gone. Dictators, despots, conquerors still march across the pages of history, and each has his little day.

But of the Babe who was born in Bethlehem, God Himself has told us: "He shall be great and shall be called the Son of the Highest . . . and of *His* kingdom there shall be no end." (Luke 1:32, 33)

Small wonder that from millions of hearts and voices and from unnumbered "kindreds and tongues and people and nations" there still comes the age-old call:

Oh, come, let us adore Him,
Christ, the Lord!

God's Broken Heart

An unbeliever was seated in the pastor's study. Although he was a sincere seeker after truth, he nevertheless found it impossible to reconcile all the wickedness and misery in the world with the Bible's doctrine of the goodness and the mercy of God.

"If God were really good, all of the misery and wickedness in the world would break His heart," he said.

"It did," replied the pastor, and then pointed to a painting of the Crucifixion on the far wall of his study.

Had you ever thought of the crucifixion in that way? As the breaking of God's heart because of the sinfulness and stubbornness of His rebellious creatures? As the breaking of God's heart because of *your* shameful record of disobedience and transgression?

In a very real sense the story of the suffering and death of Jesus Christ, our Lord, is the story of the breaking heart of God — breaking because of the world's iniquity.

The Scriptures tell us that God loved the world so much — this world of misery and wickedness — that He willingly surrendered, sacrificed, gave up, His only-begotten Son — to suffer and to die in the place of fallen sinners.

And of this Son, who had lived with the Father, eternal in the heavens, the Scriptures tell us: "He is despised and rejected of men, a man of sorrows and acquainted with grief. . . . But He was wounded for our transgressions, He was bruised for our iniquities; the chastisement of our peace was upon Him, and with His stripes we are healed." (Is. 53:3, 5)

In a pre-eminent sense it is true that when cruel hands nailed our Savior to His cross, God was there! God was there fashioning the salvation of a world of misery and wickedness. For "God was *in* Christ, reconciling the world unto Himself, not imputing their trespasses unto them. . . . For He hath made Him to be sin for us who knew no sin, that we might be made the righteousness of God in Him." (2 Cor. 5:19, 21)

Yes, on that first Good Friday the heart of God did break for your sins and for mine. Will we bring Him *our* broken hearts, broken in contrition and repentance, in return?

My Father Understands

Little Jimmy had just spilled some paint on the back porch. He had tried not to, but he *did!*

"What will your father say?" asked his frightened playmate. "Aw — he'll understand," was Jimmy's confident reply. And little Jimmy was right. His father did "understand" and willingly forgave him.

After all, who understands us better than our father or our mother? Who is more ready to forgive us when we fail, or to cover our shortcomings with the mantle of sweet charity?

The father heart remembers the limitations of the child — and in that remembrance is moved to love and pity.

So, too, our *heavenly* Father. The psalmist says: "He hath not dealt with us after our sins nor rewarded us according to our iniquities. For as the heaven is high above the earth, so great is His mercy toward them that fear Him. . . .

"As far as the east is from the west, so far hath He removed our transgressions from us. Like as a father pitieth his children, so the Lord pitieth them that fear Him. For He knoweth our frame; He remembereth that we are dust." (Ps. 103:10-14)

He knoweth our frame — that we are so weak, so erring, so sinful. That is why He offers us a salvation that is full and *free,* dependent upon no merit of our own.

In Christ and His atoning work we have everything that the loving Father heart of God could give: forgiveness of sins today and every day, and eternal life with God in the everlasting mansions.

What peace, what joy, what confidence — to know that in heaven we have *such* a Father, a Father who understands, who knows us by our very names, and who, knowing us, forgives us!

Our Pledge of Life Eternal

Men of all ages have sought for pledges of immortality — for proofs of a life beyond the grave. In our day it has become fashionable to point, for instance, to the dying leaves of autumn and to the tender shoots of springtime as pictures of human death and resurrection — and as pledges of a life beyond the tomb.

But when the cold fingers of icy death come tapping on our shoulder, there will be no comfort in the fact that October is the time of falling leaves and that springtime is the season when the lilacs and the lilies bloom!

At that moment nothing less will comfort our turbulent souls than the vision of our Savior, triumphant in the skies, with the seal of victory over death in His nail-pierced hands and the shout of assurance on His lips: *"Because I live, ye shall live also!"* (John 14:19)

His victory over the grave is our pledge of life eternal. His empty tomb proclaims to us that someday our grave, too, shall be empty. "Christ is the First Fruits of them that slept" (1 Cor. 15:20), says Paul. Just as the first fruits are the foretaste, the forepledge, of a later and more general harvest, so Christ's resurrection is the guarantee and forepledge of our resurrection to life eternal — in that later, greater harvest.

For us death holds no terror. Our mighty Champion has gone before us, through the valley of the shadow, preparing the way that we might follow. He has lifted the veiling cloud which hung heavily over what seemed to be the journey's end — and at the top of the road that winds up the far side of the valley we see our Father's house with all its many mansions!

His glorious resurrection on that first Easter morning is our pledge of life eternal.

> He lives and grants me daily breath;
> He lives, and I shall conquer death;
> He lives my mansion to prepare;
> He lives to bring me safely there.

Are We Getting Ready?

Little Margie came home from Sunday school and said to her mother: "Mamma, teacher told us today that God puts people into this world so that they can get ready for heaven."

Almost without thinking, the mother replied as she tested the roast in the oven: "Yes, dear, that's right."

Wrinkling her little forehead into a thoughtful frown, Margie hesitated a moment and then asked in all seriousness: "Then why don't we see anybody getting ready?"

A childlike question! And yet, in a very real sense, how true! "If God puts people into this world so that they can get ready for heaven, then why don't we see anybody getting ready?"

In the hurry and the hubbub of our busy world people have become so preoccupied with the affairs of the day, with the pressing problems of this world, that many of them have forgotten all about "getting ready" for the *next* world.

And yet the psalmist tells us: "Thou carriest them away as with a flood. . . . They are like grass. In the morning it flourisheth and groweth up; in the evening it is cut down and withereth." (Ps. 90:5, 6)

Surely, we have every reason to continue with the Psalmist and pray: "So teach us to number our days that we may apply our hearts unto wisdom." (Ps. 90:12)

In other words, teach us to "get ready." Teach us to regard this life only as a period of preparation for a greater and much more wonderful life which is still to come — the life with Thee and all of Thy redeemed in heaven. And teach us to employ our days, our years, so that they might stretch out in the sure direction of our heavenly home.

Are we doing that? Are we really "getting ready"? Do we daily confess our sins to God, our Father, and pray Him in Jesus' name to forgive us? Have we rested our entire case, for time and for eternity, in the hands of Jesus, who is mightily able to save to the uttermost them that come to God by Him?

Then, in the words of little Margie, we are ready.

He Knew the Shepherd

It happened many years ago. A group of well-educated people were gathered at the home of a friend for a sociable evening. Among them was a popular actor of the day.

During the course of the evening the actor was asked to give a reading, and he obliged by reading the Twenty-third Psalm. All were impressed by his deep, rich voice, his clear enunciation, and the rhythmic rise and fall of the well-measured tones as they came from his lips. Here indeed was an artist!

After he had finished, the group asked an elderly clergyman to read the psalm. Timidly he declined. But he asked permission to explain certain of its verses, both against their historical and geographical background and in the light of their New Testament fulfillment in Jesus, the Good Shepherd.

As the clergyman expounded the beautiful psalm, he became more and more absorbed in its message, completely forgetting himself in the process. And at the end, almost involuntarily, he quoted the entire psalm — as the humble confession of his believing heart.

Particularly moving was the confidence with which he repeated the words: "Yea, though I walk through the valley of the shadow of death, I will fear no evil; for Thou art with me; Thy rod and Thy staff, they comfort me."

The light of faith shone in his eyes as he concluded: "Surely, goodness and mercy shall follow me all the days of my life, and I will dwell in the house of the Lord forever."

A hush fell over the group as the elderly clergyman sat down. There had been a difference in the two readings, of which they were all aware. And yet — just what *was* the difference?

Later that evening one of the company put his finger on the difference when he was heard to observe: "The actor knew the Shepherd's Psalm, but the pastor knew the Shepherd."

More to Follow

The story is told of a well-to-do man who died, having left detailed instructions as to the disposition of his wealth. Among other things, his wife was to turn over a certain sum of money to a poor minister who had frequently remembered the family with deeds of kindness.

The widow thought it would be best to turn the money over to the minister a little at a time, in regular installments; so she mailed him $25, and inside the envelope she placed a slip of paper upon which was written: "More to follow."

Every two weeks, without fail, the elderly man would find the identical amount of money in his mailbox with the identical message: "More to follow."

"More to follow!" That is Christ's unbreakable pledge to all who believe in Him. The blessings which we receive today are but a pledge of those which we shall receive tomorrow; and those we receive tomorrow will bear the pledge of heaven: "More to follow." His mercies are new every morning. His compassions fail not.

The evangelist John, in his Gospel, speaks of the inexhaustible riches of Christ and says: "Of His fullness have all we received — and grace for grace" (John 1:16). Literally, "grace *upon* grace." Christ's goodness pours in upon us as the waves of the sea. As the one comes, there is always another close behind, and then another and another. "Grace upon grace." Christ's capacity and willingness to supply our needs, both spiritual and material, are unlimited and eternal.

There is no need in our life, however great or small, that Christ does not know and which He will not fill, if it be necessary for our eternal welfare. "My God will supply *all* that you need from His glorious resources in Christ Jesus," says Paul. (Phil. 4:19, Phillips)

Surely, we who have such a bountiful Savior need never fear that His grace and goodness may ultimately run out. From His hand we have received, and we shall continue to receive, "grace upon grace." From His inexhaustible spiritual resources, as long as heaven and earth shall last, there shall always be "more to follow."

That Sand in Our Shoe!

A man who had hitchhiked from coast to coast, and who had walked many miles in the process, was asked what he had found the most difficult to endure.

To the surprise of his questioner it was not the steep mountains or the dazzling sun or the scorching desert heat that had troubled him, but — in the words of the traveler — "it was the sand in my shoes."

Frequently it is the little things in life that make the practice of the Christian faith most difficult. Somehow the great trials of life — moments of crisis, of serious illness, of death and bereavement — have a way of raising us to higher levels and bringing us closer to the only Source of spiritual strength, namely, our Savior, Jesus Christ.

But those *smaller* trials! How they plague us! And how they succeed again and again in causing us to fall and stumble! Those little irritations in the home, those endless vexations at the shop or office, those little rubs with the neighbors, those petty quarrels at the church — those are the "sand in our shoe" which wear us down and which frequently wear our Christianity thin.

And yet we know that they *shouldn't*. It is particularly in coping with these "sand in the shoe" vexations that we Christians are to cultivate that Christlike charity which "suffereth long and is kind" (1 Cor. 13:4).

It is in the way that we handle these smaller but more persistent irritations that we show our Christian forbearance — or our lack of it.

But where get the grace, the spiritual power, to cope with these exasperating vexations? Only from Him who has asked us to "follow Him" — our great Exemplar of patience and forbearance. Only he who has learned to walk with Christ, every hour, every moment of the day, will learn to take life's hour-by-hour irritations in his stride.

Have we been permitting "little things" to get us down? to destroy our family happiness? to sour our dispositions? to cause us to sin against our loved ones and, above all, against the Lord of Glory who has bought us?

Then let us pray for pardon in the Savior's name — and for a greater measure of that love which suffereth long and is always kind.

Is There a "Marble" in Your Life?

Little Billy was terribly frightened. He had put his fist into his mother's expensive narrow-necked vase and was unable to pull it out again.

Unable to help him, his mother had called the neighbors and informed them of the youngster's plight. Eager to be of help, the man next door had hurried over and had worked with Billy for nearly ten minutes, trying to extricate his little fist — but to no avail.

Finally someone asked the lad if he had opened his fist inside the vase, thus narrowing the size of his hand so that it could be withdrawn more easily. "Oh, no!" the tearful youngster sobbed. "Then I'd lose my marble!"

There are many people much older than little Billy who are just as foolish. They want everything that the Christian religion has to offer — the forgiveness of God, the peace and contentment which come from Christian faith, the assurance of eternal life with God in heaven — but they don't want to let go of the "marble" in their hand.

That "marble" may be sinful pride; it may be selfishness; it may be self-righteousness; it may be luxury; it may be the love of money; it may be evil associations and wicked companionships; it may be any one of a thousand different things which stand between a man and fellowship with God.

The tragic fact is, they don't want to let go of these things! Like little Billy they refuse to open their hand lest they lose their precious treasure, and in so doing they jeopardize their soul's salvation.

Is there a "marble" in your life that you should have let go of long ago? Some besetting sin which you have never ceased to coddle and which is putting your spiritual life into jeopardy?

The Bible tells us what to do with every evil that our hands might still be clutching. "Let us strip off everything that hinders us, as well as the sin which dogs our feet, and let us run the race . . . our eyes fixed on Jesus, the Source and the Goal of our faith." (Heb. 12:1, Phillips)

Let us get rid of that marble in our hand!

Greater Than the H-Bomb

It was the great Sir James Simpson, world-famous scientist, who, when he was asked, "What do you consider your greatest discovery?" replied: "That I am a sinner and that Christ is my Savior."

In a day of hydrogen bombs and sputniks, this "greatest discovery" may not seem to be of much importance. And yet it is the greatest discovery that any man can make.

Within the reach of every one of us God has placed a power which can spell the difference between heaven and hell. This power was made available to us on a little hill outside the city of Jerusalem some 1,900 years ago. There the powers of heaven met the powers of hell, and the powers of hell were vanquished.

When the Son of God, our Savior, died in the place of sinners, the infernal power of Satan was forever broken, and the "power of God unto salvation" was let loose upon the earth. That is what Paul calls the Gospel of Christ — *"the power of God* unto salvation to everyone that believeth." (Rom. 1:16)

Millions of people down through the centuries have attested to the new power which entered and cleansed and redeemed their lives, once they put their trust in the message of the Cross. And millions living today can bear witness to that power.

The paramount question in your life and mine is "Have we personally made this great discovery? Have we made personal contact with the power of Christ's Cross?" We can do so by simply receiving Him into our lives as Savior and Lord.

The Bible tells us: "As many as received Him, to them gave He *power* to become the sons of God, even to them that believe on His name." (John 1:12)

In an age of H-bombs and man-made satellites, Sir James Simpson's personal discovery still remains the greatest — "that I am a sinner and that Christ is my Savior."

Have we made that discovery?

Send for Me!

A young man, working in a large factory, was spending his first day on a new job. Everything went well until shortly after noon, when the machine which he was operating began to make an unusual sound.

Eager to demonstrate his mechanical ability, he began to tinker with the machine — with the result that it soon came to a complete stop. Nothing that he could do would start the wheels in motion again.

Just then the foreman walked up. The young man, somewhat embarrassed, but still trying to explain and defend his actions, told his superior exactly what he had done and then, shrugging his shoulders, added: "After all, I did my best."

"Young man," the seasoned foreman replied, as he looked the precocious novice squarely in the eye, "around here, doing your best is to send for me!"

What a lesson in life!

"Doing your best is to send for me!" How often has our heavenly Father had to remind us of that humbling yet strengthening fact! In our foolish pride we sometimes think that we are doing our best when we apply our own puny wisdom to the difficult problems of daily living; and we forget that in the vexing trials and temptations of the Christian life "doing our best is to send for Him."

"Call upon Me" (Ps. 50:15) is still God's command and invitation to all His children. "I will deliver thee" is still His promise. "And thou shalt glorify Me" is still His holy expectation.

How often each day do we really "send for" Him who has so graciously promised to help us? "Pray without ceasing " (1 Thess. 5:17), the Scriptures admonish us. "Pray constantly," a more modern version has it.

Our Lord in heaven would have us know that none of us is doing his best who is not sending for *Him* every moment of the day.

But He would have us know also that those who do make a habit of sending for Him will surely do their best — as He measures "best."

The Long Look of Lent

After the assassination of Abraham Lincoln, while his body lay in state, a great procession of mourners passed by his casket. In the vast throng was an elderly Negro woman together with her four-year-old grandson who held tightly to her hand.

As they came up to the bier of the great emancipator, the aged woman stood motionless for a long moment, looking at the lifeless form of her slain benefactor — hot tears running down her cheek.

Then she stooped and lifted the little boy so that he, too, could see the body of the dead President. Wiping the tears from her eyes, she said to the lad: "Honey, take a long look at that man. He died for you."

Indeed, he had done just that! He had given his life so that little lad — and millions of others like him — might live their lives in dignity and freedom. And, as few other men that lad would ever see, he deserved "a long look."

In an unspeakably higher sense the Christian world is pausing during these days to take "a long look" at the One who gave His life that *all* men might be free — free not from an earthly taskmaster but from the slavery of sin, death, and the power of the devil.

The Man on the Cross who engages our attention during these days is none other than the Son of God, who loved us and gave Himself for us — the Lenten Lamb who bled and died so that we might be forever free from the guilt, the power, and the punishment of sin. He died for *us!* He died "for *our sins*," the Scriptures tell us. (1 Cor. 15:3)

How important that each of us find time for the long and quiet look of reverent contemplation! Not just a passing glance, but a long and thoughtful look! The look of penitence. The look of faith. The look of gratitude. The look of love. The look of unconditional self-surrender.

> Behold the Savior of mankind
> Nailed to the shameful tree!
> How vast the love that Him inclined
> To bleed and die for thee!

His Face Upon Us

It was well past midnight. Little Ronnie, who had been asleep for hours, suddenly awoke in the midst of a bad dream. Not knowing whether he was alone in the dark bedroom, he whispered in a trembling voice: "Daddy, are you there?"

From across the bedroom came the reassuring voice: "Yes, Ronnie, Daddy's here." For a minute Ronnie lay silent, still not quite sure that his bad dream had not been real. Once more he whispered: "Daddy, and is your face toward me?"

"Yes, my face is toward your bed."

And with that assurance the little fellow closed his eyes and drifted back to slumber. His father was with him, and his father's face was toward his bed.

What a picture of the child of God and his relation to his heavenly Father! The child of God knows that "the eyes of the Lord are upon the righteous, and His ears are open unto their cry." (Ps. 34:15)

Often our lives become so tangled, our minds so weighted with worry and anxiety, our nerves so ragged, that we are almost afraid to face life another day. It is especially at such moments that we must remind ourselves that God is with us in the darkness and that His face is always "toward" us.

As we look out into the black night of the years which lie before us and our hearts begin to fill with fear, let us find strength and comfort in the immovable assurance that God is already in those years. He is already in 1965 and 1970 — and when *we* get there, we shall find His eyes are still upon us.

And through Christ, we know, His eyes are the eyes of love, of tenderness, and of deep compassion. Because of what the Savior did for us — in Bethlehem, on Calvary's cross, in Joseph's tomb — God has turned His face toward us!

As day after day we leave the old behind us and step into the new, let us pray: *The Lord bless us and keep us; the Lord make His face shine upon us and be gracious unto us; the Lord lift up His countenance upon us and give us peace. Amen.*

"You Can Tell He's Been There"

The lecturer had completed his fascinating travelog, and one woman was heard to say to another: "I always like to hear him describe a country. You can tell that he's been *there*." Together with others, she had been impressed by the authority with which he spoke and by the unimpeachable, first-hand knowledge which lay behind his every utterance.

Somehow we feel that the faithful few must have felt the same way about every reference of the Savior to the homeland from which He had come and to which He would soon return. Whenever He spoke about His "Father's house," He spoke with the authority and the certainty of One who had been *there!*

No one can read the account of His midnight inter-view with Nicodemus, for instance, without being im-pressed with the clarity, the certainty, and the finality with which He spoke of the things of heaven. "We speak that we do *know* and testify that we have *seen*." (John 3:11)

And no one could have witnessed that tender scene in the Upper Room when the Savior spoke fondly of His Father's house to His disciples without sensing the Savior's intimate and accurate knowledge of the "house" of which He spoke. Remember the absolute assurance with which He spoke? "If it were not so, I would have told you." He knew, and He knew very well, because He had been *there!*

As one who stands on a mountaintop — looking down into the valley beyond and telling his comrades behind him what he sees — so the Savior tells us about His Father's house and ours. The streets of the eternal city are familiar to Him, the mansions of the Father's house stand clear and bright before His eye. He *knows* what lies beyond the valley, for He has *come* from there.

That is why He can say with an assurance which in the case of any other would have been proud presumption: "If it were *not* so, I would have *told* you!"

What a comfort, to have as our dearest Friend Him who has already spent endless ages in the eternal Father's house, who knows the way, and who by His glorious redemption on Calvary's cross has opened up that way for us.

Thank God that the eternal Guide into whose hand we have placed our own is thoroughly acquainted with the mansions of the Father. Acquainted — because before the world's foundation He had already *been* there!

Prayers Without Words

Little George Henry was having difficulty saying his prayers. The three-year-old had struggled manfully with some of the "big words" in the new prayer his mother was trying to teach him, but somehow the words just weren't suited to his little lips.

After repeated attempts — all of them futile — he decided that he had done his best. Taking a deep breath, he rattled his way through a string of unintelligible sounds and then confidently assured his mother: "Jesus can make a pray out of that!"

We don't know how his mother answered him, but there is at least one sense in which his unexpected remark was right. Jesus *can* make prayers out of our wordless supplications, and He can answer them before we find the words to give them utterance.

In his Letter to the Romans Paul tells us: "Likewise the Spirit helps us in our weakness; for we do not know how to pray as we ought, but the Spirit Himself intercedes for us with sighs too deep for words" (Rom. 8:26 RSV). In other words, God's Holy Spirit knows the inmost wishes of our heart, even those which we cannot put into words, and He carries those unspoken wishes before the Throne of Grace.

Sometimes we are prone to judge the power of a prayer by the beauty of its prose, by its measured cadences, or even by the eloquence of him who speaks it.

Of course, there is nothing wrong in sending our petitions heavenward in the very best language at our command, especially if our prayers are spoken in public worship. Our God deserves the best we have — also in the language with which we approach Him.

But it is not the language that determines the power of the prayer! It is rather the Spirit of God, who occupies our heart and who knows our inmost wants and wishes and who bears those wishes to the throne above "with sighs too deep for words." It is God Himself, through His Holy Spirit, who can take our wordless sobs and give them wings and send them soaring to the heavens. It is He who can "make a pray" out of our most inarticulate groanings.

Let us keep our hearts open to His Holy Spirit!

> For He can plead for me with sighings
> That are unspeakable to lips like mine;
> He bids me pray with earnest cryings,
> Bears witness with my soul that I am Thine,
> Joint heir with Christ, and thus may dare to say:
> "O heavenly Father! hear me when I pray."

The Oldest Company

It happened at the noonday luncheon of the local Rotary. The dishes had been cleared away, and the meeting had been called to order.

After the reception of new members and the introduction of visitors, the chairman asked who of those present represented the oldest company in the community.

A young man in the back of the room hesitated a moment, then arose and said: "I believe I do, sir, I am a minister of the Gospel. The company I represent was founded some 1,900 years ago. And I am happy to say that it is still flourishing."

His announcement was greeted with applause, for none of those present was inclined to contradict him. He did indeed represent the oldest company in the community. And, what is more, everyone agreed that his company was still a going concern.

It was nineteen centuries ago that the Founder of this company had said: "Upon this rock I will build My church, and the gates of hell shall not prevail against it" (Matt. 16:18). How true the intervening centuries have proved His startling prediction to be!

On every continent and on the islands of the seven seas, from east to west, from north to south, the company of Christ's redeemed have carried the message of salvation, until today there are some 900,000,000 people

scattered over the face of the globe who claim membership in that blessed company! What a glorious band!

> Elect from every nation,
> Yet one o'er all the earth,
> Her charter of salvation:
> One Lord, one faith, one birth.
> One holy name she blesses,
> Partakes one holy food,
> And to one hope she presses,
> With every grace endued.

It was that "company" that the young minister represented — indeed the oldest, grandest, and the largest to
be represented at the meeting. And it is to that "company" that you and I belong through faith in Christ, the
Savior.

Are we always conscious of the glorious fellowship
we have by virtue of our membership in the company
of Christ? We are "fellow citizens with the saints and
members of the household of God, built upon the foundation of the apostles and prophets, Jesus Christ Himself
being the chief Cornerstone." (Eph. 2:19, 20)

Thank God — that is the company to which we
belong!

The Word for the Moment

Bishop Taylor was one of the chiefs of chaplains in the English army during the First World War. It is said that he applied a simple test to all British clergymen who volunteered to serve as army chaplains during that conflict.

Holding his open watch in his hand, the Bishop would say to each volunteer: "I am a dying soldier. I have only one minute to live. What must I do to be saved?"

If during the ensuing minutes the applicant would say: "Believe on the Lord Jesus Christ, and thou shalt be saved," or words to that effect, he would be accepted. If he gave any other answer, he was rejected.

Whatever else may be said of the Bishop's test, surely he knew the only availing message in the moment of death! In that moment nothing but the divine assurance of full, free, and final forgiveness through Jesus Christ, our Savior, will bring peace to our anxious soul.

No pious platitudes, no honeyed words about a God "in general" who loves the world "in general" and who will take the human race "in general" to some "beautiful isle of somewhere" will bring strength to our step as we walk into the valley of the shadow.

Above all, no attempt to draw comfort from our own past record of achievement — our own goodness, our own virtue — will bring light into the gathering darkness of that moment. No one will know better than we that our own righteousnesses have been as filthy rags. (Is. 64:6)

The word for that moment will be, always and only: "Believe on the Lord Jesus Christ, and thou shalt be saved." (Acts 16:31)

Believe that God in His mercy sent His Son to be your Savior and that on the altar of the cross His Son atoned for your entire guilty record. Believe that in Jesus Christ you have a Savior-Shepherd who gave His life for you and has promised to guide you safely through the dark valley of death to the bright mansions of His Father.

Millions who have stood at the door of death and have crossed its threshold will attest that this was "the word for the moment."

Big Brothers

$\mathbf{I}$t is a familiar sight to see
a carefree little two-year-old venturing boldly forth
from the safety of his father's house — and then, all
unknown behind him, to see "big brother," who has
been sent by a loving father to see that no harm befalls
the little one.

The Bible tells us that our Father's house above is
filled with legions of "big brothers" — His holy angels
— whose constant duty it is to guard and keep us on
our way. It is of these big brothers in our heavenly
Father's house of which the Scriptures ask:

"Are they not all ministering spirits, sent forth to
minister for them who shall be heirs of salvation?"
(Heb. 1:14). And, again, speaking of these heaven-
sent guardians, the Scriptures say: "He shall give His
angels charge over thee to keep thee in all thy ways.
They shall bear thee up in their hands lest thou dash
thy foot against a stone." (Ps. 91:11, 12)

How often in the midst of grave perils, when dangers
threatened within and without, has our soul been
strengthened by the assurance that one of our "big
brothers" was walking at our side. How often, after
a night of dark and anxious hours, have we been able
to greet the new morning with the words of Daniel on
our lips: "My God hath sent His angel and hath shut

the lions' mouths that they have not hurt me." (Dan. 6:22)

What comfort for us who are "the children of God by faith in Christ Jesus" to know that — no matter what the circumstances of life — our heavenly Father has sent a bigger, stronger brother to stand guard over us and to deliver us from every evil!

Let us be done with doubt and fear. Let us venture forth upon our daily tasks, confident of His loving and divine protection. And at the end of the day, when we close our eyes in sleep, let us commend ourselves to His keeping with the quiet prayer:

> Lord Jesus, who dost love me,
> Oh, spread Thy wings above me,
> And shield me from alarm!
> Though Satan would devour me,
> Let ANGEL GUARDS sing o'er me:
> "This child of God shall meet no harm!"

It Was Only a Slum Mission

It was only a slum mission on a side street in the poorer section of town. Freshly painted and clean, it stood out in striking contrast to the crumbling buildings and disorderly storefronts which surrounded it.

Over its humble entrance, painted in black letters on a white board, was the simple sentence: "We Preach Christ Crucified."

We had, of course, read that sentence a hundred times before. We had heard it in sermons, read it in tracts, seen it on bulletin boards, and had ourselves used it again and again in our own conversation.

But somehow this evening the words took on new meaning. As they spoke to us from the crudely painted sign board, they seemed like an echo out of the distant past. Nearly 2,000 years ago the apostle Paul had written these identical words to a mission in the godless city of Corinth.

To them, and to all who would read his letter, he wrote: "We preach Christ crucified — unto the Jews a stumbling block and unto the Greeks foolishness; but unto them which are called, both Jews and Greeks, Christ the Power of God and the Wisdom of God." (1 Cor. 1:23, 24)

With that simple but Heaven-sent message a scattered group of little "missions" was destined to turn the world upside down for Christ. For the very power of God was in that message! (Rom. 1:16)

They preached not only Christ — but *Christ crucified*. Not only Christ the great prophet, the great teacher, the great regilious leader — but Christ the Sin-Bearer, the Substitute, the Sin-Atoner, the Mediator, "the Lamb of God which taketh away the sin of the world." (John 1:29)

And *that* was the message which, according to the sign board over its entrance, was to be proclaimed to the humble folk who would gather that evening in the mission we were passing.

Fortunate people, we mused! More fortunate than thousands who would gather tomorrow in splendid cathedrals from whose pulpits the Gospel of the crucified Christ would not be heard.

It was only a slum mission, but if it remained faithful to the signboard above its door, it could be the gate of heaven for all who entered.

Sunset and Sunrise

We were flying due west — far above the horizon-to-horizon carpeting provided by a layer of fleecy white clouds a thousand feet beneath us.

As the early evening hours wore on, the soft carpet behind us gradually turned into a bluish gray — its far edges blending silently into the darkness of approaching night.

The long stretch of downy carpet which still lay ahead was spectacularly bright — splashed with a riot of brilliant color.

In the distance ahead of us the blood-red sun was slipping beneath the billowy clouds — painting the floor beneath us, first gold, then red, and then a deepening purple.

In a few moments the sun was gone, and the carpet of clouds beneath us gradually disappeared from view. All was inky darkness. As we leaned back in our seat in the plane, we mused on the sermon of the sunset. For every sunset *does* preach a sermon to the believing heart.

> Beyond the sunset,
> O blissful morning,
> When with our Savior
> Heav'n is begun,
> Earth's toiling ended!

[224]

O glorious dawning
Beyond the sunset,
When day is done!

Beyond the sunset
No clouds will gather,
No storms will threaten,
No fears annoy.
O day of gladness,
O day unending,
Beyond the sunset
Eternal joy!

Beyond the sunset,
O glad reunion
With our dear loved ones
Who've gone before!
In that fair homeland
We'll know no parting —
Beyond the sunset
Forevermore.

The plane sped on into the night. As we looked out into the gathering darkness, we realized that the miracle we had just witnessed had been both a sunset and a sunrise — for the same sun which had just slipped beneath the far horizon had, at that very same moment, risen upon a new morning in a land beyond our view.

To the heart which has found eternal life in Jesus Christ, the Savior, the end of "life's little day" is both a sunset and sunrise — ushering him into the light of God's *eternal* day.

Topical Index

[229]